How
God
Speaks
to Us
Today

By Rosalind Rinker:

The Years That Count
Prayer: Conversing With God
Who Is This Man
You Can Witness With Confidence
The Open Heart
Communicating Love Through Prayer
Praying Together
Conversational Prayer
Within the Circle
Sharing God's Love
Making Family Devotions a Priority
Ask Me, Lord, I Want to Say Yes
Learning to Pray (With Cassette)
How to Get the Most Out of Your Prayer Life
How God Speaks to Us Today

Rosalind Rinker

How God Speaks to Us Today

Fleming H. Revell Company
Old Tappan, New Jersey

Library of Congress Cataloging in Publication Data

Rinker, Rosalind.
   How God speaks to us today.

   1. Christian life—1960-   . 2. God.
3. Rinker, Rosalind. I. Title.
BV4501.2.R556   1985   231.7′4   84-17948
ISBN 0-8007-1414-8

Speak, Lord, for Thy servant heareth.

Mary . . . sat at Jesus' feet
          and heard His word.

My sheep hear My voice,
and they follow me.

Contents

Preface

The subject of hearing God speak has been a familiar one in most of my writings. Now I have practically written an autobiography of the important decisions of my life and how God spoke and led me to delight in His will.

But this contains one difference: In my other books I have written about how we can talk to God; here I wrote about how and why God talks to us.

I gratefully acknowledge the help of my typists, Jean West and Marge Reinhold; and of Connie Warren, who prepared the Appendix.

Mostly I am filled with grateful thanks to the Holy Spirit, who again and again came to my assistance in instructing me what to include and in refreshing my memory.

ROSALIND RINKER
2400/3A Mariposa West
Laguna Hills, CA 92653

How
God
Speaks
to Us
Today

Part I

God Wants to Speak to Us

A relationship exists between hearing God speak to you and the depth of your personal willingness to do His will. In other words, to be totally committed to hearing His voice, to abiding in Him, and to believing on Him whom He has sent, even Jesus Christ our Lord, these are the marks of true discipleship.

In the parable of the sower (Mark 4) again and again our Lord emphasizes the importance of hearing. "He who has ears to hear, let him hear" (4:9 RSV). How we hear and what we do with what we have heard result in the fruit bearing in our lives.

Consider these two qualities in the life of Jesus:

1. *Communication with His Father:* "Father, I thank you for having heard me. I know that you always hear me . . ." (John 11:41, 42 NAB).
2. *His personal commitment:* In the Garden of Gethsemane, Jesus prayed, "Father, if it is your will,

take this cup from me; yet not my will but yours be done" (Luke 22:42 NAB).
2. "My food is to do the will of Him Who sent Me, and to accomplish His work" (John 4:34 NAS).

Part I explores several main avenues through which God speaks to us. We start with His written Word (the Old and New Testaments) and the Living Word (Jesus Christ, our Lord, who speaks to us from the pages of the Holy Bible and in our hearts, through His Spirit).

Then, having hidden His words in our hearts by reading, by meditation, and by memorizing, God speaks to us through countless other avenues and brings up from our subconscious minds that which is relevant to our needs or situations. He does this through circumstances, other people, even our own desires and our prejudices, in order to bring us to full discipleship, which means delighting in His will and obeying His Word.

God Speaks to Us Through Everything

Everything that He has created in the heavens and the earth

Everything that is contained in the Holy Bible, the Word of God

Everything in the Old Testament and the New Testament

Everything that happens to you and to me: past, present, future

Everything that does not happen to us

Everything: good or bad, failure or success, death or life

God is speaking to us,
>   all the time,
>   all the time,
>   all the time.

1

God Speaks to Us Through His Word

I'd like to start this chapter with a true story my secretary, Jean, told me about her eleven-year-old daughter, Stephanie.

One morning Stephanie brought her Bible to her mother, with shining eyes full of excitement.

"Look, Mother, what the Lord said to me this morning!" With her finger on the page, Stephanie proceeded to read the verses following the Lord's prayer: "For if you forgive men their trespasses, your heavenly Father also will forgive you; but if you do not forgive their trespasses, neither will your Father forgive your trespasses" (Matthew 6:14, 15 RSV).

"That means *me*," she continued. "That means I must forgive Julie for what she did to me, and when I read that verse, I did forgive her, and then God forgave me. Oh, Mother, God does speak to people when they read the Bible, doesn't He?"

17

Forgiveness Means Freedom

A recent *Time* magazine cover story focused on Pope John Paul's forgiving the man who tried to assassinate him, "The Pope pardons the gunman," reads the caption. No one ever expected to see such an article in *Time,* with such strong pleas for forgiveness addressed to nations in conflict today. The piece closes with this sentence, "Forgiveness does not look much like a tool for survival in a bad world, but that is what it is."

Stephanie freed not only herself, but also her little friend. Pope John Paul freed himself and Agca, the gunman, by that God-inspired act of forgiveness. Neither would have forgiven had not God spoken to them.

From the beginning of time, forgiveness was given to Adam and Eve in the Garden, but with penalties that have plagued mankind ever since. Stop to think about it for a moment. Think of the Bible stories you can remember and the part love and forgiveness played in all of them. Man's prejudices, which spring out of his pride, his lusts, and un- filled desires, produce the need for love and forgiveness. Only the word of the Lord and the power of the Spirit can induce a person to love when he has been injured.

While you are thinking about that, remember that sin is missing the mark, the mark or ideal for which God created us. Sin brought disease and death to our planet. Jesus was a sent one; He was the Word made flesh, to give His own body as a remedy for sin. I don't understand it all, but I believe it, and there is peace within. Even before Christ came, God spoke to the patriarchs and began to lay down the pattern for the events of the New Testament.

God Spoke to Abraham

We sometimes get lost in narrative details and fail to pin down the main object of a story. Think of the story of Abraham. Why did God speak to him? How often did Abraham miss the mark? And how often did God forgive him? God wanted a people for Himself, who would worship and love and obey Him, upon whom He could pour His multitude of blessings.

Last year someone lent me a storybook about Abraham, and after reading about half the book, I became aware that the author had given us a picture of a man plagued by doubt and questions. *Why give so much space to that subject?* I wondered. Had not God spoken, even in an audible voice, and given him directions regarding his family and his future?

Suddenly I saw what the author had not written down: Abraham did not have what we have today. He went through long periods of time when there was no communication, no word from the Lord. He had no Bible, no Psalms, no promises written down, no miracle accounts of men and women who had obeyed God, no one to talk with who also knew the true God. (No TV, no radio!)

Turn to the eleventh chapter of Hebrews, and read the list of Old Testament characters to whom God spoke. Abraham receives a prominent place in that roster of faith.

God Spoke to Moses

Moses is another who has been given a prominent share of that eleventh chapter. Rereading his story (which I've known for years!) I saw something I'd never noticed before. Read it for yourself in Exodus 3. Moses was tending the flock of his father-in-law in the wilderness, when he saw a bush burning, yet the fire did not consume it. When the Lord saw that Moses paused, looked, stood still, and waited, it was then that the man heard, "Moses, Moses," and answered, "Here am I."

If Moses had kept on walking past that burning bush, if he had not stopped and stood still, what then?

Moses did stop. God did speak and reveal His plan, which was to end the oppression of His people in Egypt. Abraham listened, even to being willing to sacrifice his only son, Isaac. Countless others in the Old Testament could be named, and in each case there was both a heart willingness to hear, and a commitment to do the will of Jehovah-God.

New Testament Hearers

God's plan is more clearly revealed when Jesus Christ comes to our world. He is spoken of as "the Word" sent directly from the Father.

In the beginning was the Word, and the Word was with God, and the Word was God.... And the Word became flesh and dwelt among us, full of

grace and truth; we have beheld his glory, glory as
of the only Son from the Father.

John 1:1, 14 RSV

Long ago God spoke in many different ways to
our fathers through the prophets [in visions,
dreams, and even face-to-face], telling them little
by little about his plans. But now in these days he
has spoken to us through his Son to whom he has
given everything, and through whom he made the
world and everything there is.

Hebrews 1:1, 2 TLB

In Mark's Gospel, a good half of the fourth chapter is
given to Jesus' parable of the sower. The seed that was sown
in various kinds of ground (which symbolizes our hearts)
was *the Word,* and the emphasis is on *hearing that Word* in
order to have a good harvest, or a life filled with meaning.

"Jesus Christ is the same yesterday and today and for
ever" (Hebrews 13:8 RSV). He is still speaking to us through
the written Word of God, and through His indwelling Spirit,
that Word becomes a lamp to our feet.

In the Gospels many joyfully heard the word of the Lord,
even though they did not understand. Like the young virgin
Mary, who accepted the message and gave us the Magnificat
(Luke 1:46–55). Like Joseph, her betrothed, who, after a few
questions, also accepted. Like the disciples, who left all to
follow the call of Jesus.

The Acts of the Apostles is filled with accounts of others
who heard and obeyed the Lord. But not always were people ready to hear and to obey; it tells of cases like Saul (later

the Apostle Paul), who went about hauling believers to prison and death for what he believed to be heresy (Acts 19:1-31; 22:4-16; 26:9-18), or Peter, whose dietary religious practices conflicted with the message God was giving to him (Acts 10; Romans 1:28, 29).

In both cases, God sent strong circumstantial evidence that they were unable to gainsay, and in the end both men obeyed the Lord. They did not understand what God was doing, but they knew He spoke. The Holy Spirit revealed to them that the Gentiles were to be included as well as the Jews in the benefits of Christ's death and resurrection.

Today's Hearers of the Word

Does God speak in an audible voice? There are those who will tell you that He did speak to them so. Sometimes the inner voice of the Spirit is so clear that one almost seems to hear it physically.

The Spirit, who speaks to us through the written Word, is the special gift of the Father and the Son, given at Pentecost. Jesus' teaching on the work and the person of the Holy Spirit is found mainly in John's Gospel, chapters 14-17.

There are more people studying and reading the Bible today than in any period of the existence of the church. Bible Study Fellowship, started by Wetherell Johnson, a British missionary once in China, is attended by thousands of women every week (especially in the western United States), and many of them are unchurched. Men's classes have also sprung up.

Various organizations reaching college students have a

structured Bible-study program that goes into three levels.

Churches of all denominations are in a state of renewal, largely due to the charismatic influence that has brought a hunger to know the Word of God. *How to Read and Pray the Bible* and books of like titles, in which the authors bring a fresh approach can now be found all over, including Catholic bookstores.

With all the easily understood translations and paraphrases of the Bible available today, what valid excuse do we have?

God is speaking to you in this *now* moment. Let your heart answer Him, for you are precious in His eyes, and His everlasting love always surrounds you.

Chapter Review

1. Name two qualities in the life of Jesus, which we also need.
2. Name several methods God uses to speak to us today.
3. What conditions did Abraham and Moses fulfill in order to hear God speak?
4. When did you last share a verse with someone, after having your own daily devotions?
5. What is the Spirit saying to you, after reading this chapter?

For Meditation

MY PRAYER: "Open thou mine eyes, that I may behold wondrous things out of thy law" (Psalms 119:18).

JESUS' ANSWER:	"Then opened he their understanding, that they might understand the scriptures" (Luke 24:45).
JESUS' PROMISE:	". . . The Comforter, which is the Holy Ghost, whom the Father will send in my name . . . shall teach you all things . . ." (John 14:26).
PAUL'S PRAYER:	". . . The God of our Lord Jesus Christ . . . give unto you the spirit of wisdom and revelation in the knowledge of him: The eyes of your understanding being enlightened . . ." (Ephesians 1:17, 18).

2

God Speaks to Us Through His Holy Spirit

When the Spirit of truth comes.... He will glorify me, for he will take what is mine and declare it to you.

John 16:13, 14 RSV

... The Counselor, the Holy Spirit, whom the Father will send in my name, he will teach you all things, and bring to your remembrance all that I have said to you.

John 14:26 RSV

Since we are plainly told the Holy Spirit will remind us and teach us all that Jesus wants us to know, it behooves us to be open to the Spirit and to know when He is speaking to us.

This chapter will deal mainly with how the Spirit speaks to us and how He sorts out the other voices that clamor within us. Chapter 12 will go into the fruits and gifts of the Spirit and answer questions many have about their personal relationship to the Holy Spirit.

During one period in my life, I felt very confused about the Holy Spirit, but evidently that did not hinder Him, for at every turn He guided and taught me, often when I did not recognize Him. How faithful is the love of God! We are guided by as much truth and light as we have accepted and gently (or not gently) led on to more truth.

Who Is the Holy Spirit?

Much of my confusion was cleared up by meeting people filled or baptized with the Holy Spirit, as I saw them personify the love of Christ.

Then my fears dissolved like snow in the sun when I discovered 2 Corinthians 3:15–18. Paul speaks of the veil of unbelief (or lack of knowledge) that lies over the minds of people until the Spirit of the Lord removes it, so that with unveiled faces we behold "the glory of the Lord, [and] are being changed into his likeness from one degree of glory to another; for this comes from *the Lord who is the Spirit*" (3:18 RSV, *italics mine*).

Jesus Christ is the Holy Spirit—blessed holy truth to which I was blind for more than thirty years. I never gave the Holy Spirit the worship, the honor, the adoration that is due Him. The Holy Spirit is, in truth, our own Lord Jesus returning in spirit to live within us as He promised. This is one of the mysteries of our faith.

What Does the Holy Spirit Do?

1. The Holy Spirit speaks to us, revealing the Person of Jesus Christ
2. He reveals the will of God in our lives and affairs
3. He opens the Bible, so we can understand it
4. He opens our ears to hear His voice
5. He helps us distinguish the other voices within us
6. He shows us that our hearts need cleansing
7. He is the agent God uses for that cleansing
8. He gives us both the fruits of the Spirit and the gifts of the Spirit
9. He changes us so that we become Christlike in loving and forgiving one another

How Does the Holy Spirit Work Within Us?

This is a great mystery to many, but to those whose hearts have been opened, it is a continuing revelation. The more we cooperate with the Holy Spirit, the more He can guide us.

The Spirit has to put up with all the eccentricities of human nature, but how does He bear our ignorance of the Word of God? The Bible is our reliable guidebook to discerning the will of God and the basic truths governing our lives. However, when we do not put that Word into our minds (into our subconscious selves), how can the Spirit, who is God's operator or programmer, call it out into being?

Our minds act something like computers: If nothing is there, there is nothing to work on. A computer can only put out what has been put into it, so if we put confused messages into it, we will get confused messages out of it. Programmers call that *GIGO,* meaning "garbage in, garbage out."

Garbage coming out of the lives of God's children can only mean they are listening to wrong voices, and there are many. The Holy Spirit alone truly guides, the others mix truth and error—enough truth to make it acceptable and enough error to lead us in the wrong direction.

Here is a test we can always use to be sure the Holy Spirit, and not some other spirit, is speaking to us: *Does this exalt and glorify the Lord Jesus Christ? (see* John 16:13, 14).

Is the Holy Spirit your programmer? Or are you trying to run the show yourself? If you are, the wrong information may be filling your mind.

So often I hear someone say, "I would give anything to be able to hear God speaking to me." Or again, "I thought God was speaking to me, but it didn't work out." Or even, "The Man upstairs must not be at home; I don't get any answer."

Today's seekers lack three things:

1. Knowledge about the true character of God
2. Knowledge about who they really are
3. Inability to discern the voices that come to them

The Holy Spirit has been given to guide you into these truths, for the truth sets you free. Proper information puts your mind into positive gear, so the Spirit can speak to you and guide you into that good and acceptable will of God.

The more you learn, through reading the Bible, the more your heart will yield to and trust the loving-kindness of God and the better able you will be to distinguish between the voice of the Holy Spirit and the voices Satan uses to deceive you.

The Character of God.   Just as we come to know people through being with them and watching them live through their relationships with others, so we can come to know what to expect from them. In the same way we can know what God is like.

The written Word reveals God through His *servants:*

David reveals the warm tender compassionate forgiving nature of Jehovah as no other writer has. The Psalms have become our prayer book.

Isaiah writes of God's judgments upon His people for not hearing His voice, but in the latter chapters (40–65) he gives us the other side of the coin. He tells us that our Maker is our husband, that He will comfort us, help us, never forsake us, listen to our cries, and be with us in all our adversities. Knowing our human weaknesses and contradictions, He still calls on His people to open their ears, listen to Him, and obey His voice.

In the *New Testament* God is revealed through His Son, Jesus Christ, who plainly told His disciples, "He who has seen Me, has seen the Father. I

and My Father are one." His compassionate love
for sinners was balanced by His discernment of hy-
pocrisy, which He severely denounced.

We can trust Him in every crisis, for our God never
changes. He is the same, yesterday, today, and forever.

Know Who You Really Are.   You are made in the image
of the Lord God.

Your spirit needs to be re-created in the image of God,
because when sin came into our world, we were all contami-
nated.

The clearest passage in the Bible about this is found in
Romans 5. I recommend you read it in *The Living Bible,*
which makes this difficult truth easier to read and to understand. The gist of that chapter: As by one man, Adam, sin
came into the world, so by one man, Jesus, forgiveness and
mercy and acquittal came for all who will receive this free
gift.

We call this being "born again," and a person feels just
that way (regardless of those who spoil the term for us).

There is a difference between knowing *about* Jesus and
knowing *Him.* That happened to me when I was fifteen
years old, and it changed the course of my life.

> I know who I am.
> I know to whom I belong.
> I am God's child,
> Loved and protected by Him,
> Actually indwelt by Him,

Like the branch in the vine.

I know who I am
I know to whom I belong.

After more than fifty years of walking with Jesus, I still want to know more about Him. His Word is a lamp unto my feet and a delight to my heart. He is my Beloved, and I am His.

Discerning the Voices That Come to Us.   There may be more than three sources, but for simplicity we will use the following:

1. The voice of the Holy Spirit, which is also the voice of the Father and of the Son
2. The voice of Satan, that great deceiver who uses enough truth to make the error attractive
3. The voices of our own personality, which Transactional Analysis (TA) has broken into three parts: the Parent, the Adult and the Child

The Voice of the Spirit.   In this chapter we have already outlined who He is, what He does, how He works within us, and the rest of this book will continue to enlarge on the practical ways by which He guides us. The Holy Spirit never speaks of Himself or on His own authority; He always speaks of Jesus and makes His Person, His ways, and His will known to those with ears to hear.

The Voice of the Deceiver.   Peter cautions us, ". . . Be watchful. Your adversary the devil prowls around like a roaring lion, seeking someone to devour. Resist him, firm in your faith . . ." (1 Peter 5:8, 9 RSV). Jesus taught, ". . . The devil . . . has nothing to do with the truth, because there is no truth in him. When he lies, he speaks according to his own nature, for he is a liar and the father of lies" (John 8:44 RSV).

Jesus also taught, ". . . My sheep hear my voice. . . . A stranger they will not follow, but they will flee from him. . . ." (John 10:27, 5 RSV).

The deceiver will use the voices of your own personality to confuse you, while the Holy Spirit will also use the same voices to give you His guidance. How does one tell the difference? I've found that God is never in a hurry, while Satan pushes me. God's way is always the way of love and sometimes it's tough love.

The Voices of My Own Personality.   When we speak of the various voices within us we seldom are aware of who is speaking, or we quickly put them into two familiar categories: Either it is the Lord or Satan leading us away from the Lord.

Have you considered the three parts of your own personality? Through reading the following books, I've become better acquainted with myself: *When God Says You're OK* by Jon Tal Murphree (Inter-Varsity Press), which is the Christian viewpoint of the secular book *I'm OK—You're OK* by Thomas A. Harris.

Most of the problems or decisions in my life finally center

around loving God and loving people, or being successful, and here are some of the questions I ask myself:

Questions and Prayers

Is this the voice of the *spontaneous child* within me, wanting my own way? Or is it the *mature adult* who is willing to accept the responsibility of his or her choice? Or could it be the *strict parent* who wants to keep me in line with God's accepted behavior?

Added to the above, comes the voice of the deceiver who clouds the whole issue. Then is when I take refuge in the Word of the Lord. My favorite verse (for prayer) for years has been Psalms 27:11: "Teach me thy way, O Lord, and lead me in a plain path because of mine enemies."

Teach me Thy way, O Lord
Lord, I know Your way is best.
I lay mine at Your feet.
You are Lord of my life, of my affections,
    of all my comings and goings.
I only want to be taught.
Teach me, Lord Jesus, by any method You choose.

Lead me in a plain path
The path seems to be in confusion right now.
Please end the conflict.
Open my ears to hear Your voice.
Open my eyes to see Your path.
Lord, is this Your path for me now?

Lead me and I'll follow.
Please make it plain.

Because of mine enemies
Lord, my enemies are not flesh and blood.
They are my own natural desires to belong,
   to love and to be loved.
Have mercy on me.
Teach me Thy way.
I am easily deceived by my own feelings.
Lead me in a plain path.

The Desirable, Seductive Tone

The deception is that the tone of the tempter may be nice and even desirably seductive, but the content, time, place and person are wrong.

Praying about an illustration to use regarding such temptations, I discarded quite a few. After talking and praying with some of my disciples, we felt that one of the most common and subtlest problems deceiving people today is that of "having an affair."

The older I am, the more I am in touch with people, the more I realize that in our private lives there are struggles that we seldom share. The one I refer to, "having an affair" can be defined as "having sex outside of marriage." Whether based on love or lust, the end result breaks God's laws and it breaks us too.

What begins with good feelings ends with guilt, despair

and depression. However, we have a great God and a great Savior, who redeems everything. Let us remember following Jesus includes suffering and pain, and there are many varieties.

The Mentality Within Us

Here is an example in the forefront of today's life-styles, the "if it feels good, do it" mentality that deceives and infests all walks of life. Even the believer is not exempt.

CHILD: I'm crazy about so-and-so. I'm really in love this time. I can even do my work better.

PARENT: You've said that before. You know it is against God's law. You are only getting into more trouble.

ADULT: The choice is mine, and this time I'm getting what I want. I'm not hurting anybody else.

EVIL VOICE: Didn't God make you like that? So why not enjoy yourself? You deserve to be loved like this.

GOOD VOICE: You are the Lord's child, and He calls you to holiness, and to take up your cross, to avoid the temptation and to follow Him—not to gratify the desires of the flesh.

So How Is the Conflict Resolved?

It is a delusion to think that Christians live in a perpetual rose garden. The surrendered life, the yielded life is no accident, but a series of deliberate choices. Read the eighth chapter of Romans.

Even as I continue to pray Psalms 27:11, the way of deliverance is usually "hitting the bottom" with grief before I rise to learn anything of value. But the outcome is worth it: I am delivered from judgmentalism. I have mercy for my fellowmen, I am quicker to lay down my own desires and feelings at the feet of Jesus and to make decisions according to His will, instead of letting circumstances work themselves out.

Making Decisions

It is in the making of decisions that the difference is apparent. Decisions like:

1. Following Jesus as Lord in obedience.
2. Looking for a spiritual director to counsel and pray with, in all situations—meaning: oral confession, restitution as guided, and report on obedience.
3. For me: A decision for celibacy based on loving the Lord, my God, with all my heart has become my life-style, which means loving Jesus and letting Him live out His life within me.
4. That in turn helps me live out Peter's exhortation: "Seeing ye have purified your souls in obeying the truth through the Spirit unto unfeigned love of the

brethren, see that ye love one another with a pure heart
fervently " (1 Peter 1:22).

Chapter Review

1. Read 2 Corinthians 3:15–18, and yield yourself
   anew in praise to Christ.
2. Turn to the page listing the nine things the Holy
   Spirit does for us. Check the ones you would like to
   have operate more freely in your life.
3. How does the Holy Spirit speak to us? What is a
   good test?
4. What three things hinder us most when it comes to
   hearing God speak? Select one that seems to influence you most and pray about it.
5. When did you come to know who you really are?
6. Which of the three-in-one persons within you influences you the most?
7. What is God's remedy or checks-and-balances sys-
   tem to keep us walking in the light?

3

God Speaks to Us Through One Another

In the first chapter, we saw that God does speak to individuals. Somewhere in the hours between writing, something interesting occurred to me. I became aware that while the messages God gave these people involved their own lives, they were not primarily for themselves alone.

Abraham's obedience to the Lord had far-reaching effects: He became the father of the great nation of Israel. Moses' obedience resulted in the emancipation of Israel and later his bringing the laws of God to the people.

So hearing and obeying the Lord has two dimensions: first, that of immediate personal blessing, given to the one who hears; second (and perhaps even more important), the continued communal blessing received by those who hear as the message is passed on.

Hearing Has Two Dimensions

Because of the implications of the personal blessing and the passed-on blessing, we need to think and meditate more on what the Lord has said to us and our obedience to that word, for we are one Body, and each member contributes to the health and welfare of the whole.

A clear example of this principle is found in the account of the conversion of the Apostle Paul. To get the entire story, you need to read three portions of Scripture, for in some of them Paul becomes more explicit: Acts 9:1–18; 22:4–16; 26:9–18.

After the light from heaven struck Saul to the ground, this conversation took place:

> "Saul, Saul, why do you persecute me?"
> "Who are you, Lord?"
> And he said, "I am Jesus, whom you are persecuting."
>
> Acts 9:4, 5 RSV

After that, Saul was instructed to go to Damascus, and there he would be told all that would be appointed for him to do.

The scene now shifts to the conversation between the Lord and Ananias, for he was the one appointed (or chosen or selected) to tell Saul (who later became Paul).

Ananias strongly objected to the idea of going to see this man, for it could cost him his very life. How could he take that risk?

"Go, for he is a chosen instrument of mine to
carry my name before the Gentiles and kings and
the sons of Israel; for I will show him how much he
must suffer for the sake of my name."

Acts 9:15, 16 RSV

Here we have the two dimensions again. Saul's personal
life was changed, his name was changed, his lifework was
changed, but the benefits and blessings of Paul's life and
subsequent ministry and letters to the churches will always
be a great part of the bulwark of truth that every Christian
embraces. We Gentiles have become in a sense "completed
Jews," which means the wild olive branch is flourishing as
part of the original olive tree (Judaism) (Romans 2:29;
11:17–20). Paul still speaks to us through his letters in the
New Testament.

God Wants to Speak to Us Through One Another

After considering the material you have just read, I'd like
to ask you to sit down and trace the relationship in your own
life between knowing what God wanted you to do and how
it came about and tracing the far-reaching results later in the
lives of others.

I tried it first and took a sheet of paper and began at my
conversion, which came about because a stranger invited me
to accept Jesus as my Savior. I wanted to, and I did.

Very quickly, as I wrote, I saw that within a period of ten
or twelve years, I had six incidents written down. I was

amazed that I had never before related cause and effect in my own history.

Since this is not a detailed story of my life, I will be content with sharing just one of those incidents, for it concerns the writing of my books.

God's Message Comes to Me

I was fifteen years old at the time of my conversion, and in five years I was in China as a secretary for missionaries. As a young missionary, I often wrote for the *Standard,* published by the Oriental Missionary Society, but usually only when I was invited to do so. I also remember that the letters I wrote back home (to North Dakota) were always published in the *New Rockford Transcript* and read by the whole county. I expect my father being states attorney had something to do with that. At any rate, I got a start, but I didn't do much else.

I remember Mrs. Charles B. Cowman (president of our mission and author of *Streams in the Desert*) asking me many times, "Rosalind, when are you going to use that gift God has given to you?"

I would always reply, "When the Lord opens the door." For only then would I know how and where to use it. That sentence could be the motto of my life, for whenever I have tried to force any door open, nothing happens. When I wait for the Lord, the door stands open.

The China years rolled on, and I watched the Lord open the way for me to study the language and then to go with a team of young women into rural areas to teach and evangelize.

The Right Door Opened

In order to follow through on God's opening the door to a writing career, I will skip over a few years—those when China closed and my fourteen years as a counselor of college students with Inter-Varsity Christian Fellowship. That time brought enrichment and depth and experience.

The right door to writing was opened by God through a friend, and soon invitations for holding workshops followed. Here is how it happened: Eugenia Price asked me to accompany her to Forest Home, a mountain resort in southern California, where she was the speaker for the week.

After she met with the committee, I remember her coming into the cabin and sitting down rather heavily, as if she bore a great load. She did. "They not only want me to speak to adults, but to juniors, to high schoolers and college students! What shall I do? I only know how to speak to their neurotic parents!"

I gave Genie a pencil and paper and proceeded to outline a long list of subjects that interested youth and that I knew she would handle very well.

At the close of that week, she said, "Ros, that was a terrific list you gave me. What are you doing with all that material? It ought to be in a book so everybody could use it."

She had already published several books, so Genie called and told Zondervan publishers she was sending a friend to see them, one who had a message that should be in a book.

The editorial committee really rolled out the red carpet for me that day. It was decided that my first book would be for young people, as I had just completed fourteen years with IVCF. At once they brought out a contract, and I signed it. Mind you, they had not seen even one sentence I'd written, let alone a whole manuscript.

During the ensuing years, fourteen books have been published, with millions of copies now in circulation. Eight of them have been translated into eleven languages. They mainly deal with devotion and discipleship to Jesus Christ, through love and meaningful prayer. The vehicle for this has been Conversational Prayer, which I define as two or more praying in dialogue on one subject at a time, with simplicity, honesty, and faith.

A Recent Experience

This more recent experience carries out our theme of God speaking through a friend and the concept of answered prayer. Ten years ago, when I moved from the cold winters of Chicago to Southern California, I hesitated for several long months before making the move. Ruth W., who prays for me, knew of my hesitation and finally wrote and told me to go ahead and put into action the plan in my mind. She was right, and her concern and prayers helped me.

The first year I spent quietly in the desert. Then for two reasons it seemed right to move into the Los Angeles area: my telephone bills were too high (all my friends lived there) and plane connections from Los Angeles International Airport were better. But where would I live? If it was right for me, surely the Lord had a place for me.

Sharing this concern and prayer item with my longtime China friend, Mildred Rice, we discussed it and prayed about it. She came up with this suggestion, "Why not live in Leisure World? It is a protected community, and you won't have stuff stolen from your home, as you did in Chicago, when you were out in meetings."

I liked the idea, but there was one objection: I was unable to purchase an apartment or manor. Mildred quickly put me at ease by telling me there were always a few for rent and that if the Lord wanted me there, the door would open. I agreed at once. (That magic phrase!)

I rented the most reasonable one I could find, and I've been here more than ten years. It is larger than I need, but provides an office for both myself and my part-time secretary. I'm on the third floor, and as I type I look out on several tall palm trees and the distant Saddleback Mountains.

Does the Lord care where you live? He certainly does. Ask me. I'm only half a block from Clubhouse 4, where there is a heated Olympic-size pool, plus a Jacuzzi, and an art room, where I've picked up oil painting as a hobby. I've made some good friends, and I'm at home in the will of the Lord.

Best of all, is the way the Lord put me here through Mildred's suggestion, though she did not know that someday my landlord and his wife would become partners with me in the ministry to which God has called me. Mr. and Mrs. Haugen live in Glendale, owners of a large drugstore there.

How are they my partners? This came about after I gave them a few of my books and we had some talks on the telephone. I am practically a guest in this lovely apartment, which I could not otherwise afford. I pay a very moderate rent, which enables me to live comfortably in this beautiful area, thanks to the Haugens and to the Lord, who planned it all.

I believe that all things come from the hand of our Lord and that nothing is too large nor too small for His attention.

This Lord is also your Lord, and He will do the same for you.

God does speak to us through our friends who love and pray for us, and He uses us to speak to them, too.

Dependence Upon Others

While I am grateful for the love and concern of others, I have learned that I must confirm that guidance within my own spirit and not without haste.

I am exceedingly wary of just anyone coming to me announcing that he or she has the word or the will of God for my situation. Manipulation of the sacred words "the will of the Lord" is frequently practiced without insight to know the danger that exists.

May the Lord have mercy upon us all and prevent us from falling into that bondage which demands explicit confirmation from others. It is the Holy Spirit within who brings trust and peace and ability to discern. God can give to each one of us the discernment to know the difference between manipulation for power and concern because of love.

Chapter Review

1. Spend a few moments quietly in God's presence. Is there anyone who needs a call or a letter from you?

2. Meditate on obedience and trace the effects of your own obedience in the lives of others.
3. "Ask and you shall receive." Ask the Lord to give you a prayer partner, that together you may channel His power to others.
4. Turn to the Appendix and pray over that list, writing the names of people who come to you during that time. Pray for God's timing in your contacting them.

He who has ears to hear, let him hear.

Mark 4:9 RSV

4

God Speaks to Us
Through Our Desires

Trust in the Lord, and do good; so you will
dwell in the land, and enjoy security. Take delight
in the Lord, and he will give you the desires of
your heart.

Psalms 37:3, 4 RSV

As a teenager I memorized those verses in the King James
Version, and while security meant nothing to me at that
time, the desires of my heart certainly did.

What are the desires of a teenager? Or of any of us as the
years stretch into responsible adulthood and then into the
not-so-golden years. Our dreams strongly relate to our iden-
tities.

For the disciples of Jesus, there should be no problem
about who we are. We know we are the children of God and

47

that, following Jesus, we are led into His plans for us. Thus does life become both meaningful and useful.

Yet for many Christians the questions remain:

Who am I?
Why was I ever born?
What can I do to make people aware of me?
What makes me different from others?
What is the meaning of life?

The answers to those questions can be found as we develop two qualities that mark the life of our Lord: Jesus listened to His Father speak and had a total commitment to His will. These are available to every one of us, if we hear His voice. Making them the aim of our lives will take care of the desires of our hearts and at the same time provide the much needed security.

What of dreams thwarted or gone awry? One of my lifelong friends lost a dear grandson, a student in a Christian college, where he took his own life. What were his desires? Was he unable or unwilling or perhaps even ashamed to share them with anyone? Or was some part of life just too much for him?

Suicide is an intolerable burden for loved ones to bear. Many reliable teachers of the Bible believe that when one of God's children is pushed beyond the limit and takes his own life, he has passed the limit of responsibility. We believe the atonement of Christ takes care of this, that we will meet them again in eternity.

We must be committed to loving one another, which

means we become aware of even the unspoken burdens of those persons in our immediate circle. Even when normal desires are exaggerated beyond control, sharing and praying will help bring balance.

Normal Desires

Normal desires are those which are common to the human race, not all of which are fulfilled in the lifespan of every individual. We could put them into two categories: physical and psychological needs. Which do you think are the most vital for you? Which influences you the most?

Since the mind controls the body, let's consider the psychological needs. That inner part of us which we will say includes the spirit and the heart and all its desires has three basic requirements:

The need to love and be loved
The need for security
The need to feel that we are worthwhile to ourselves and to others

This description comes from *Reality Therapy,* by William Glasser, and I haven't seen a more concise one.

The Need to Be Loved. Recently I have been corresponding with a young woman who, having reached the age of twenty-nine, felt she was losing all hopes of finding the right man to be her husband. Did God's plan for her include marrying a man who loved her, having a home and family

of her own? She opened her heart and shared deeply with
me.

After praying over her letter several days, I wrote urging
her to have patience, to believe that God loves her and does
have a plan for her, that the most important part she had to
do right at this time was to say a great big *yes, Lord,* deep in
her heart and wait.

Yes, Lord, means, "Whatever your plan is, dear Lord, I'm
willing—whether it means what I want or what I don't
want."

In a few months another letter came, this one full of hope
and joy because she had met a young man, was already
sharing many things with him and looking forward to what
might come next. She was full of questions, but a different
kind from those in her first letter.

Her chief concern was that prayer would be answered and
that they might become good friends before they became
lovers.

God speaks to us through our desires, then as we lay them
at His feet, He helps us sort them out and quiets our hearts
to accept what He has already prepared.

The Need to Feel Worthwhile.   Just as the Father plans
for our emotional needs and pours His love into us in order
that we may love one another, it follows that, being loved,
we begin to feel worthwhile. Such love frees us to explore
the whole area of being useful, of doing some kind of work
that in the end supports us and that we feel happy doing,
which in turn leads to the security we need.

Young people sometimes have a hard time knowing just

what they want to do. Others seem to know instinctively; most student nurses, for instance, have known for years that they wanted to be in nursing.

I have a friend who told me that her first teacher in Chinese brush painting never once commended her work, and she did miserably. She tried another teacher, who praised every good stroke she made. Now she is doing various kinds of beautiful Chinese art.

In a sense, we are our brother's keeper, and we can call forth one another's gifts and help one another find the life-work God intended for us.

Desires God Rechannels

After careful reading and meditation, the verses from Psalm 37 take on an enlarged meaning. They not only declare "God will give you the desires of *your* heart," they also imply that the desires that are coming into your heart are not your own; God gives them to you.

God rechannels our desires for our good and for His own purposes. Only then do real fulfillment and peace come to one's spirit. This took place in the life of Jesus on earth, so those who follow Him find their strength and confidence anchored in Him alone.

> ... Holy Father, keep them in thy name, which thou hast given me, that they may be one, even as we are one. ... that the love with which thou hast loved me may be in them, and I in them.
>
> John 17:11, 26 RSV

The Desires God Gives

For God to give me His desires meant first of all that my love had to be rechanneled away from myself and some dreamed-of person, to Jesus Christ Himself. The hurts and disappointments in that process led me straight to the artesian fountain of water Jesus spoke of in John 4:13, 14.

In contrast to the earth water, which continually makes one thirsty without quenching that thirst, Jesus invited me to drink of the water He gives, for He declared, "Whosoever drinketh of the water that I give him shall never thirst." The earth water includes all that human love and security can provide, while the water Jesus gives is the Holy Spirit, who is the source of all love, including love's gifts and love's fruits.

When God says no or denies me something that others have (earth water) like a husband, a family, a home, and children, I know that He has planned something better for me and for His own purposes.

This has been true through the years, though the commitment is a difficult one and often needs to be repeated. In God's plan He has given me good friends all over the world, plus children in the Lord.

In a sense my fifteen books are my children, and they bring me new grandchildren all the time, as those who are helped write, asking for prayer and for caring. I have already told you about my present home in Leisure World, which provides the (earthly) security I need right now.

My Present Desires

More than anything else, I desire a few friends who love Jesus Christ and with whom I can share His love and fresh teachings. Another desire is to be ready for any invitation that comes to me to hold prayer workshops, teaching the power of prayer through prayer partners.

Wherever I have lived, God has given me a few friends with whom I can pray, talk, and share a meal or even theater tickets. Last but not least is to have the privilege to call and share God's blessings right on the telephone.

All these things are being given to me right here and now, and I want to share a special story with you about how God gives and then takes away.

After moving into Leisure World, I was invited by several local churches to conduct prayer workshops. I noticed two women who showed up at six of these meetings. Of course I met them and found they, too, lived in Leisure World. Florence Norton lived in the building right next to me, and Nellie Sillers about ten minutes from me.

Then someone told me that these two women had started a Conversational Prayer group in Nellie's home. I called on the telephone at once to thank them and was invited to join them the next Friday morning. Little did I dream that that group would become a strong prayer support for the next six years of my ministry in most of the United States.

Then the Lord slipped in something special for me: Nellie became my prayer partner, and each morning at 8:00 A.M. we shared requests and answers to prayer. This helped me become aware of the need of using my telephone to call others as the Lord put the desire into my heart.

During the writing of the first draft of this book, Nellie called asking if I could go with her to see Frances (a member of our Friday group). Frances had just called and thought she might be dying.

I left my typewriter at once and met Nellie at Frances's home. We found she needed visitors, she needed prayer, she needed breakfast and a few other things. We took care of those needs, knowing that one of these days she could quietly slip away from us. Little did I dream that, within six months, five of that Friday group would go Home to be with the Lord.

The Very Next Day

Nor did I dream that the next one to go Home would be Nellie. The following morning we prayed about a meeting where I was speaking that day.

I arrived home from that workshop about 4:00 P.M. I rested and about 6:00 P.M. felt prompted to call Nellie and share how God answered our prayers. At first I resisted, thinking I would wait till the next day, but I couldn't seem to put it off.

We had only been speaking for less than ten minutes when suddenly there was no response, either to my statements or to my questions. Tragedy struck quickly. I heard only silence and heavy breathing. Immediately I called the paramedics (always on duty around here) and also a member of our group.

When I arrived at Nellie's home, the ambulance was just leaving for the hospital. Nellie had suffered a massive stroke and was partially conscious for only a few moments. She held my hand tightly as I prayed and repeated the Twenty-third Psalm, one we said aloud every time we drove anywhere in the car.

Our prayer group surrounded her with the healing light and love of Jesus, but two days later Nellie slipped Home to be with her Lord and her loved ones. The gift God had given her was one of "helps." She was available anytime for anyone who needed a ride to the doctor's or to market.

The Lord was guiding me more than I knew. What if I had not made that 6:00 P.M. phone call?

I affirm: I believe that the desires God gives us in our hearts are the ones He wants us to act upon. Yes, even to keeping in touch with others by telephone.

Invitation to Desire

The inner spirit is a very private one and responds only to a gentle person whose ears have been opened to the voice of the great lover, our Lord Jesus.

God, our Father, is saying to us the words He said to the three disciples at the time of the transfiguration of our Lord:

> . . . This is my beloved Son, with whom I am well pleased; listen to him.
>
> Matthew 17:5 RSV

Jesus Himself invites us:

Come.... learn of me....
Matthew 11:28, 29

Deny yourself, take up your cross and follow me.
See Mark 8:34, 35

... Love one another; as I have loved you....
John 13:34

See Appendix for a longer list of the invitations given to us as His disciples.

Chapter Review

1. Memorize Psalms 37:3, 4. Write it on a slip of paper and carry it with you. Meditate upon it.
2. Give thanks to the Lord for the way He has fulfilled your normal desires.
3. Which desires has He rechanneled? Give thanks for those also.
4. As a result of reading this chapter, what new desires are coming to you?
5. As a generous, loving sign of your love and obedience to our Lord, make plans to tell another in just what ways you think he or she is a worthwhile person.

... Morning by morning ...
he wakens my ear to hear as those who are taught.
The Lord God has opened my ear,
and I was not rebellious.
Isaiah 50:4, 5 RSV

5

God Speaks to Us Through Our Disappointments

Anticipation is the forerunner of disappointment. For when did your realization ever come up to the excitement of your expectation? In other words, anticipation always seems to be greater than realization.

Can you remember the first time God taught you a great big lesson about how to handle disappointments?

Can you remember a time when you wanted to do something for the Lord, but the door never opened?

Can you remember feeling called of the Lord and being turned down by the group you wanted to work with?

No matter what your keenest disappointments have been, the Lord God is in the business of redeeming them.

You can face yours and stop chafing under the injustice of it all; it won't kill you. It will not only bring healing to your suffering spirit, but understanding for the one who let you down.

Be prepared as you read this chapter to hear what the Lord God wants to say to you, for there is freedom and rest of spirit awaiting you, plus precious teaching for which you would not otherwise be ready.

The question I hear most is, "How do I tell the difference between the voice of the Holy Spirit and what I myself want? between what God wants for me and what I want for myself, when it seems perfectly right and good."

We all daydream about what we want to happen, and in our dreams we see our desires already coming to pass. But real-life disappointments occur when some person or situation fails to meet those expectations. This may take place when our dreams or desires are in line with the will of God, yet the timing is wrong. When our dreams are not in the will of God, we discover this and adjust, or we suffer. History bears out the fact that people even end their lives because they can't face the results when their plans fail.

Again we come right up to the subject of this book: God does speak to His children, and He has given us His Holy Spirit to guide us into His ways. Our greatest need is to present our plans to our Lord, who in His love will help us to face both eventualities—success or failure. Then we wait for confirmation, for Scripture, for an open door.

Just why a loving God permits deep disappointments that shatter our spirits is a difficult subject. I can testify that it has been going through the deep waters of troubles and even failure that has taught me the most valuable lessons about myself and about God's love and His ways.

Lessons learned through disappointments often pave the way for the next thing God has planned for us, and we are ready because we have been humbled and made obedient through our suffering.

> For as the heavens are higher than the earth, so are my ways higher than your ways, and my thoughts than your thoughts.
>
> Isaiah 55:9

> Though he were a Son, yet learned he obedience by the things which he suffered.
>
> Hebrews 5:8

The rest of this chapter will bring you three stories that illustrate the teaching given above. First, the story of John Mark, then two from my own life.

The Story of John Mark

The story of John Mark is a rather scattered one through the Acts of the Apostles. Look up the following references from which I pieced this story together: Acts 12:12; 13:2–5, 13; 15:36–40.

The big disappointment in John Mark's young life came when the Apostle Paul turned him down as a teammate. He even had sharp words with Barnabas (another teammate) over John Mark. Here's the story:

John Mark came from a fine family. As a lad he and his

mother were often with Jesus and His disciples, and no doubt they witnessed many of the miracles and heard much of the teaching of Jesus.

He also knew the power of united prayer after Pentecost, for there was a prayer meeting going on right in his mother's home when one miracle happened. Peter had been arrested (Acts 12) and was in prison, and the saints met to pray that he might be delivered. Right during that prayer meeting, Peter knocked at the door, and to their joy and amazement proceeded to tell them how the angel of the Lord opened the prison doors.

We are not told how John Mark was chosen to accompany Paul and Barnabas on that first missionary journey, but it must have been a time of great anticipation, for him and his mother and all the saints who knew them.

During a time of fasting and prayer and worshiping the Lord, hands were laid upon them, setting them apart for the ministry ahead.

The next mention of John is that he assisted the team in Cyprus, but when the team moved on to Perga, in Pamphylia, John Mark left them and returned to Jerusalem.

Acts 15:36–40 gives us only a slight clue about John Mark, when Paul and Barnabas made plans for another missionary journey and Barnabas wanted to take him with them.

> But Paul thought best not to take with them one who had withdrawn from them ... and had not gone with them to the work.
>
> Acts 15:38 RSV

> But Paul didn't like that idea at all, since John
> had deserted them in Pamphylia.
>
> Acts 15:38 TLB

We are not told why he left or what took place.

Apparently Barnabas felt John Mark had learned his lesson and was ready this time, but Paul objected strenuously, with such sharp words that the team was split. Paul took Silas, and Barnabas took John Mark.

Put yourself in John Mark's place for a few moments. Had God really called him? If a man as spiritually powerful as the Apostle Paul rejected him, could he ever be "used" in the Lord's work? Was this what God wanted? Failure the second time? Did this end his calling as the Lord's messenger?

If you have ever been in a similar situation, you know something of the agony and humiliation, of the doubt, and of the disappointment John Mark suffered.

The rest of the book of Acts tells the story of Paul and Silas, and the other two are not mentioned again. However there are two more known facts about John Mark that throw some light upon the real character of this young man: John Mark wrote the second Gospel in later life, and in that Gospel he records a scene not included in the other Gospels. It is commonly agreed that he was speaking of himself. It takes place in the Garden of Gethsemane, when all the disciples forsook our Lord and fled, except for one young man who followed Him, with nothing but a linen cloth about his body; and they seized him, but he left the cloth in their hands and ran away, naked (Mark 14:51, 52).

No doubt about the love and devotion young John Mark had for Jesus. It is commonly believed that he compared what he knew with the Lord's disciple Peter, so today we have the Gospel according to Mark.

John Mark learned the hard way, through failure, disappointment, and suffering. But he was not alone, for the Lord sent Barnabas, who believed in him, chose him, encouraged him, and that was enough.

I'm sure that John Mark would agree with the following fine-tuning tests for guidance from the tape *How God Speaks,* by Loren Cunningham:

1. Is it the right and good thing to say (or do)?
2. Is it the right place?
3. Is it the right time, right sequence?
4. Is it the right person?
5. Is it the right attitude of heart?
6. Is it the right ministry?

Learning the Hard Way

My very first remembrance of anticipation being dashed to the ground in disappointment came when I was twenty-one years old, my first year in China. I contracted malaria and was sent to Mathilda Hospital on Hong Kong Peak. I think I stayed there only a week, but it felt like a long lonesome week.

I had met only one person in Hong Kong, and she worked in an office all day. Maude called on the telephone, telling me she would come and visit me on Saturday afternoon. All week I looked forward to her arrival, for everybody seemed to have visitors except me. I imagined where we would walk in the lovely garden and how we would get better acquainted.

The time came and went. My new acquaintance never showed. I walked alone in the garden and shall never forget the letdown, the aloneness, the hurt that engulfed me.

Finally in the midst of my distress I called on the Lord Jesus to help me. What did He want to teach me, to show me through this situation?

That's when I learned that every situation in my life needs to be put into God's hands first of all, and whether it works out or whether it doesn't, I must be willing. I was also rebuked, in that I was so excited about one single friendly person coming to see me that I had not even prayed about it.

I learned that I should never, in any situation, think there is only one way for God to work out His way and teach me His will. Each time it is different, but each time He wins. And I am thankful.

Disappointed in Myself

I have another story, and this time God sent me a Barnabas to help me recover. After four years in China, as a secretary for the Oriental Missionary Society, I got it into my head that I would rather be working with people, that this office work was giving me headaches, that I would certainly end up with a nervous breakdown—just like some of the other girls I'd heard about in that mission.

I came late to work, I left early, always with a bad headache. Finally, my boss called me into his office and agreed it was time for me to go on early furlough, that I wasn't strong enough for the job. He was returning to the States that summer and would bring another secretary back to take my place. I thought he was very considerate, until Esther, my good friend, who also worked in the office, lowered the boom on me. Did I really believe God wanted me in China? Did God really call me to work here? If I went home in defeat, would I ever come back? I thought long and hard about that. She was right. She prayed with me and finally gave it to me straight: "None of us think that you are having a breakdown: We all think you are just plain lazy." WOW! How's that again?

I asked the Lord to forgive me.

And I asked the girls I worked with to forgive me.

I prayed that my boss would not find anyone to take my place while he was gone.

And I applied myself, and worked long hours, and the headaches stopped, and God helped me out of that pit of failure and disappointment in myself.

Yes, I stayed. No, the boss did not find anyone to take my place. And five years later, in His own time, God opened the door for me to go into rural China and teach people about Jesus.

God's time and place were right.

The attitude of my heart was right.

The right ministry was there.

The fine-tuning tests are correct.

God gave me His "Barnabas" in my good friend, Esther Helsby Erny. He spoke to me through her.

And I was thankful.

God is almighty and yet does not despise anyone! And he is perfect in his understanding. . . .

He does not withdraw his eyes from the righ-
teous. . . .

If troubles come upon them, . . . then he takes
the trouble to point out to them the reason. . . . He
helps them hear his instruction. . . .

If they listen and obey him, then they will be
blessed. . . .

Job 36:7 RSV, 5, 8–11 TLB

Chapter Review

1. From the three stories in this chapter put a name or
   label on the mistakes made in each case.
2. Make a list of the lessons learned through those experiences.
3. Apply these positive suggestions, together with the
   fine-tuning tests to an experience of your own. How
   did God open your ears to hear? What did He teach
   you?
4. Read Psalm 136 in *The Living Bible* and give praise
   to the Lord, for who teaches like Him?

When I pray, you answer me, and encourage me
by giving me the strength I need.

Psalms 138:3 TLB

6

God Speaks to Us
Through Our Failures

In the last chapter, we went into the subject of dealing with our disappointments and how God teaches us through them. What is the difference between disappointment and failure? Webster comes to our aid:

> *Disappointment*—to fail to meet the expectation or hope of. . . .
>
> *Failure*—to leave undone, to be unsuccessful in something.

Disappointment is a buildup in one's mind, which has been dashed to the ground. Failure is the result of trying to do something and never succeeding.

When our expectations are surrendered to the Lord or prompted by His Holy Spirit, we can rest patiently for the door to open. When we proceed on our own, even if the project is a good one, we can fall into many kinds of traps: We didn't wait for the right time or we only *thought* we knew what to do or we failed to wait on the Lord as He has instructed us to do.

I'd like to share with you more about my last prayer partner, Nellie. The week before the Lord took her Home, we drove to a nice place to eat one evening, and on the way home I debated in my mind whether to ask her then or to wait. I'm glad I asked her because if I had waited there would not have been another opportunity.

Would she be willing for me to include in this book an experience she had had in attempting to follow guidance—one that had ended in failure? Her answer was, "Yes, if you think it will help someone else."

Discerning God's Voice

First ask yourself: Can a truly devoted believer, who loves the Lord Jesus, be partially deceived and think she has heard the Lord's voice—and be mistaken? If a person is truly surrendered to the Lord, can she make mistakes in hearing God speak?

The answer is, yes, she can. And the reason is that our own desires enter into our minds, plus the mixture of truth and error that the enemy subtly plants there.

Nellie's Dilemma. In Nellie's case, she wanted to obey the Lord; she wanted to do His will; she even knew what He wanted her to do, but complications set in. First, let me tell you the story, then we will see what the Lord has to teach us through it.

It had been our custom to call each other at 8:00 A.M. every morning, share the coming day's commitments, and pray for each other or any other requests.

This conversation took place about a year ago, and we had already been prayer partners for seven years.

Instead of the usual "hello," we used this greeting when we picked up the telephone receiver: "The peace of the Lord be with you, dear Ros." "And also with you, dear Nellie."

One morning we got into a long conversation. I can't remember how it got started, but it went into the subject of "the sin against the Holy Ghost," which is the only sin that will never be forgiven (Mark 3:29).

I couldn't believe my ears when Nellie admitted that she thought she had done this; she had sinned against the Holy Ghost. When I asked her what she had done, she replied that it was something she had not done, but which she felt the Lord had told her to do, and it disturbed her deeply.

I wanted to know two things that we then discussed at length. First, what was it she felt the Lord wanted her to do, and second, did she know the meaning of "sinning against the Holy Ghost."

What God Told Nellie to Do.   She felt God wanted her to stand up in the large Presbyterian church to which she belonged and give her testimony about being born again.

After she told me that much, she broke down and started to cry, so I prayed quietly and then finally asked her some questions.

"Just when would you do this?"

Her answer: "Sunday morning, during a lull in the program."

"Does your pastor give opportunity for people to do this?"

"No, he doesn't."

"Do you feel this urge every Sunday?"

"Yes, even during the week, and then when Sunday comes, I sit there tense, waiting and hoping, but I've never been able to do it."

My heart went out to her in compassion and understanding, for I knew how tenderhearted she was and how much she loved Jesus. I also knew what an impossible situation she was in and immediately trusted the Lord to give me knowledge and gentleness to help release that bondage.

"Dear Nellie, how long have you had this urge?"

"Over thirty years, in several churches."

She could hardly speak, for the dam had broken, and those were healing tears, tears for all those years when she felt she had disobeyed her Lord, yet she had never shared this with anyone before. I began to pray audibly for her.

Suddenly my heart knew what to do. I told her I was coming over to see her. I got into my car and drove over with my Bible so we could read and pray together. I claimed the promise all the way over, "where two or three are gathered in My name, there I am . . . ," and after I got there I put my arms around her and claimed it again.

Jesus was there with us.

The gist of our talk: Did she really feel that people would listen? that the pastor would be pleased? that others would come asking for help to be born again? Did she feel it was really the right time and place—during morning worship?

In all likelihood, the opposite might take place, since it was out of order and for thirty years she had not been able to do it. People might even feel sorry for her and wonder if she was in her right mind! How about giving that testimony in a Bible class where participation was encouraged? She had never thought of that.

When the Spirit of the Lord gives guidance, He also makes a way and gives courage, peace, and ability to perform.

Nellie Sillers was one of the most compassionate persons I've ever known. She was always on call, for in this retirement center, someone always needs a ride: to the doctor, to the grocery store, to the church. She was always ready to pray with anyone or visit the sick or even sit with the lonely. When her memorial service was held, the pastor repeated again and again, "Nellie Sillers was something special." Then he would relate some area of her helpfulness.

Nellie was no babe in Christ. She had received the baptism of the Spirit years ago and loved her Lord. Every morning she gave two hours of prayer and study to Him before she began her day. She never wanted to grieve the Spirit (Ephesians 4:30), but she never had the courage to do what she thought was required of her in this one instance.

Who would guess that deep within her this conflict had raged for all those years? Thank God, it was settled once and for all that day when she shared it with me and together we claimed the authority of Matthew 18:18 (a verse that we should use more than we do):

Truly, I say to you, whatever you bind on earth
shall be bound in heaven, and whatever you loose
on earth shall be loosed in heaven.

RSV

Thank God, Nellie's inner bondage to that false accusa-
tion (of having failed) was ended.

What Is the Sin Against the Holy Ghost?   Now it was time
to get our Bibles out and turn to Matthew 12:22–32. The
Pharisees who watched Jesus heal the blind and mute,
cleanse the lepers, and cast out demons, said of Him:

It is only by Beelzebul, the prince of demons,
that this man casts out demons.

Matthew 12:24 RSV

In a nutshell, the sin against the Holy Spirit is declaring
that Jesus was possessed by Satan and worked His miracles
through the power of Satan.

Such a statement was far from any idea Nellie ever had,
and she did not understand the real meaning of that Scripture. Because she failed to give her testimony in that morning worship service, she felt she had disobeyed the Lord, and
to her that was the same as sinning against the Holy Spirit.

The word of knowledge was given to me at this time to
know what was going on. Her desire to give a personal testimony was certainly from the Lord. But the timing was
wrong, the place was not right, the people were not prepared. Added to this, Nellie's motive was divided: Her false

idea of that sin hindered her from the truth and from receiving more guidance as to how to witness. She was so obsessed with that one idea, she could move in no other direction.

Our Common Enemy

That old deceiver who masquerades as an angel of light used that partial truth to put one of God's children into thirty years of bondage. That in turn kept her from having a quiet heart to worship the Lord during the morning services. She always felt she was a failure and was being disobedient.

If she were still here, I'd like to ask her if she was aware that Jesus, her great high priest, was praying for her.

Satan, our common enemy, uses seeming or real failure as a tool for discouragement and despondency and bondage. He will use a partial truth to distress us or to accuse us of not being willing to obey the voice of the Lord. Jesus called Satan a liar and the father of lies.

Our Great High Priest

Who ever faced greater failure than Jesus did?

Because Jesus was made like unto His brethren and suffered on earth, He is now our great high priest and intercedes for us, for He is able to help us, having overcome the powers of death and of darkness. He rose again and has promised life eternal to all who trust in Him (Hebrews 2:17, 18).

Which one of us has not been betrayed by a friend, by our own lack of knowledge, by circumstances beyond our control?

We, too, must share in the truth Jesus taught that a grain of wheat must fall into the ground and die; then it will bear much fruit. He has been through it all, and He is a faithful priest and a beloved friend who knows our hearts and who separates the true from the false. "So if the Son makes you free, you will be free indeed" (John 8:36 RSV).

Jesus knew Nellie's heart was right, and He also knows when your heart is right. I believe His protection is over His children, guiding them to the place of release and freedom. This He did for Nellie when He gave her a prayer partner who understood the Scriptures better than she did.

Truth Is Waiting for You

I remember once hearing someone say, "If you've never made a mistake, you'll never make anything." Having made my share of them in my life, I was encouraged.

How a believer in Christ faces failure, disobedience, and sin, is determined usually by the theology of the church to which he belongs. At least that was true of me until I had "hit the bottom" too many times. I began to search the Scriptures for myself and found what I believe is God's way out of failure.

With Christ, who lives within and strengthens me and you, we can face anything, go through it, pull out of it, and overcome it. He gives us insight into the Scriptures, into our circumstances, and pours fresh forgiveness and cleansing into our hearts. Even so, our sins and failures are doubly redeemed by teaching and maturity.

> If we confess our sins, he is faithful and just to forgive us our sins, and to cleanse us from all unrighteousness.
>
> 1 John 1:9

> Therefore confess your sins to one another, and pray for one another, that you may be healed. The prayer of a righteous man has great power in its effects.
>
> James 5:16 RSV

Chapter Review

God's School of Discipline utilizes everything, including our assets and our liabilities. This means our successes and our failures, our sins and our shortcomings, our family and our friends, our past and our present—especially failures.

I. These are some of the negative things that contribute to failure and the positive things that can make the difference.

Negative	*Positive*
a. Think I know what God wants.	Ask Him. Commit it to Him.
b. Proceed on my own.	Wait for Him.

c. Rush ahead without prayer.

Pray about it.

d. Keep it to myself.

Share with a prayer partner.

e. Keep everything secret.

Confession is God's way.

f. Quench the Spirit.

Be open to the Spirit.

g. Follow my own desires.

Bring them to Jesus.

h. Be tense and fearful.

Trust, have courage to wait.

II. Check your own situation, and face up to the truth: How are you handling your failures?

Jesus Christ is our Great Redeemer, and He will redeem any sin or mistake you have made.

See Isaiah 1:18, 19

Part II

What Are God's Priorities?

The next three chapters take up the specific areas in life which must come under God's control if one desires to be a disciple of Jesus. Love always has a plan, and God's plan is always the best. If you are a person without a plan or with a confused plan, I pray that some guidance will come to you through these pages.

Could This Be You?

Some time ago a young woman called on the telephone, asking if she could have a talk with me. First we talked about Jesus and His will, and then we talked with Him, for He knows all things and judges with great love and mercy.

Life for her was not producing what she felt it ought to. Lacking was a spirit of joy, of wanting to read her Bible, of answered prayer.

Together we talked about the three areas of her life: her vocation, her life partner, and the use of her money. Did she feel she was in God's will in these areas?

Yes, she felt God had led her into psychiatric nursing; she loved people, and she loved her work.

No, she was not married, but found herself caring too deeply for someone with whom she worked who was already married.

No, she knew that she was not giving the Lord that which belonged to Him in tithes and offerings.

Yes, she was willing to hear Him speak and to obey, for she longed for the inner rest that comes with such a total surrender. She followed through, and peace came to her.

I have experienced all three of the subjects of Part II. God does have priorities. I like to think of myself as a disciple in obedience and holiness, who has failed many times, but each time the loving-kindness and faithfulness of the Holy Spirit have brought me back to being a child in the arms of Jesus.

I have been given God's peace in my lifework, though it changed three different times, more peace in not having a life partner, and still further peace in the use of money. I have never gone into debt, and I have never borrowed. I know without a doubt that I am in the will of the Lord and hearing His voice in all these areas.

God has a plan for you. Why not ask Him and keep your heart open for what He wants to tell you. You may need to have your own "Barnabas," just as I did, to pray with you, but you will be guided just as I have been.

> And I am sure that he who began a good work in
> you will bring it to completion. . . .
> Philippians 1:6 RSV

7

First Priority:
Your Lifework

In the three careers given to me, I have been aware each time of the gentle leading of our Lord. When I have not been quick enough to hear the first time, He has spoken again. The receptive heart is known by Him.

I first remember God speaking to me through the voice of another. A young woman invited me to give my heart to Jesus Christ. The very next night I gave my life to Him. At that time God spoke through a missionary from China, who invited all youth present to stand around the altar as she prayed for us to find God's will and plan for our lives. I was fifteen years old.

Three years later, through reading the life story of J. Hudson Taylor (founder of the China Inland Mission), I knew God's will for me was in China. My whole desire was to please Him, and while I read that book, He spoke.

Then I didn't think I had any gifts to give Him, but I could talk, couldn't I? I could tell the story of Jesus and His love, and I was willing. I'll never forget the joy and assur-

ance that flooded me when I began to share with others
what God had said to me.

Exodus 19:5, 6 was given to me as a blessing and a promise. I underlined and dated those verses. Then I met missionaries who needed secretarial help, and I applied and was
accepted.

My First Career: A Missionary

In the last chapter, I related the story of my first term in
China as a secretary to a mission board, when I became disappointed with my job.

My passport said *missionary* on it. Was being a secretary
the same as being a missionary? I wasn't sure. But through
the disappointment of having to resign myself to that present job, I learned what it meant to be a pupil in God's school
of discipline.

In my heart, I knew God had called me to teach and to
work with people. For the present the message that came
from the Lord seemed to be, "Put that calling on the back
burner and let it simmer. Do what I have given you to do
right in that office. Give your best to that job, and wait for
My time."

That next step came about through no plans of mine.
Change did come, and it came through surgery, and then
God spoke again. The surgery was for a ruptured appendix,
followed by surgery for adhesions, which brought on a
blood clot, which placed me on the critical list for one week.
I remember the doctor saying to me, "Young lady, God has

given you a second chance at life. I don't know what else pulled you through."

I spent three long months of rest and recuperation in Peking. During that time I was asked to speak in one of the daily chapel services for seminary students. I was reading Oswald Chambers at that time, and used the day's reading on hearing God's voice. That did it, for we all covenanted to listen.

There it was again. "This is a good time for the break from the office to rural China and her people." How contrary human nature is! Now that the way was being opened, I had many objections.

1. I would have to find another mission to work with. Where would I go? Our mission only had positions for seminary teachers and office workers.
2. Then where would finances come from? Where would I live?
3. The hardships of village life in China came next. The Chinese speak of eating bitterness (*ku*) when going to rural areas. No running water. Houses made of dust-clay bricks filled everything with dust.

My heart and will finally surrendered in obedience when Esther (my Barnabas) prayed with me. As we prayed, I remembered that Jesus came to a world far different from His own. Any privation or suffering I could think of would never equal what He went through.

Then the miracle happened: The mission board decided

to change their policy, to keep me on as an itinerant evangelist and teacher and to give me a team of four young women from the seminary. The next five years I spent in China's villages, visiting the young churches started by our own seminary students. That is another blessed story to be told at another time.

My Second Career

When furlough time came, I went home. Almost at the same time, World War II was raging, and war broke out between China and Japan. All American missionaries or civilians went into concentration camps. A time of bitter suffering followed.

It became a time of change for me also, for being unable to return to China, God led me, through friends and circumstances, into the next phases of His will.

In my shortsightedness I thought my whole life would be given to China, but God had other plans that He did not tell me ahead of time. I learned that one's lifework changes, that obedience and faithfulness pave the way for the next step.

I was invited to spend a week in the Canadian woods with friends and visited Inter-Varsity's Campus in the Woods. There I met the director, C. Stacey Woods, who hired me for the next five years, which turned into fourteen years.

As a staff member of IVCF, I traveled through the Pacific Northwest in a small Studebaker, nurturing groups of students in secular colleges. Later I worked in New York City and New Jersey.

The students came together for training. They needed to

know how to pray together, how to study the Bible, how to witness to their faith. During these years I gathered the material now used in my workshops and books.

My Third Career

My third and probably last career—that of a free-lance writer and speaker—came about after fourteen years with IVCF. That gift of writing, dormant for so many years, was about to be called forth.

In chapter 3 I have already told how God opened the door to this career and how that desire of my heart came into being. This step of faith brought both great personal fulfillment and growth to all the readers of my books, some of whom have written to me.

Now when young people ask me what to write about, I tell them, "Write about what you know, what you have experienced, what God has taught you—not about something you don't know."

As people began to read my books prayer workshops and speaking engagements followed almost immediately. How do I get appointments? People write to me. I really prefer to speak in a parish or a church, for then the teaching is contributing to the upbuilding of that particular body of Christ as they learn to love one another through actually praying together.

In the year 1979 I spoke in forty churches a total of 103 times; in 1980 I spoke in sixty-eight churches a total of 88 times. To be honest with you, I'm slowing down at the word of the Lord, which has already come through to me, as the previous years were just as full, if not fuller. I told the Lord I would take every invitation that came to me, if I had free time. That promise led me into many interesting situations.

As I teach others to pray together in simple, open, conversational prayer, God continues to teach me.

Your Desire Versus God's Timing

How do we tell the difference between what we desire to do for God and God's best plan for us?

The voice of the Lord constantly comes to us through our own hearts and through the pages of the Bible. If we want to, we can know the will of God. However the final test for knowing we have heard His voice is one I keep repeating: Is the door wide open?

When No Door Opens. To those of you who are in special circumstances where no door for service seems to open, here is a word of comfort: Perhaps you are caring for an aged parent, are living in a retirement center, are physically handicapped, or even serving a prison sentence that seems forever. Perhaps you have worked all your life in a job you don't like. Or you may be a single parent tied down with responsibilities, or maybe you're an unmarried single with problems.

In great love, I assure you that the tender mercies of our Lord Jesus are with you now. Your first step is to give Him yourself and all you have and let Him live out His life in you, now. He will surely come through with a special message for you.

Right there where you are, you can be a witness for Jesus Christ and share the love of God with the people around you. Like William Carey, who repaired shoes for a living but whose calling was to serve the Lord, his God.

It's one thing to give one's entire life in religious service, and it's another thing to serve Him in the secular job He has given you. Acknowledge that He is with you, that you are going to serve Him just where you are, and see what happens.

The Final Test.   The final test for knowing if you are in the will of God in your lifework is to have the door swing wide open without your pushing it.

Recently I received a letter from a married woman who was quite distressed because she didn't know what the Lord had in store for her after her children grew up and left home. Should she begin now, she wanted to know, and prepare for that time? Rereading her letter, I noticed that it would be at least twelve years before her youngest would leave home.

Drawing on my own experience, plus my prayers for her, I wrote back that my best guidance for her was to leave the future in the hands of her Lord (who loves her and who knows the future) and give the very best she has right now to her family, her husband, her friends, and her church. In other words, become aware that she is serving the Lord in serving them.

Another woman wanted me to pray that God would change her husband's and pastor's mind. She felt called to witness for God by going to a South American country and there sell Bibles and distribute tracts. However, neither her husband nor her pastor believed that this was God's will for her at this time. I asked how many children she had, and she replied, "Six, between the ages of five and fifteen." When I heard that, I agreed with her husband and her pastor. I counseled her to trust God for a quiet heart to do what He had already given her to do, right there in her own home, and not to look for greener pastures until His time came.

If you are feeling dissatisfied and longing for a greater place of usefulness, read Isaiah 40–65 in *The Living Bible* and mark all the wonderful promises of God's love and faithfulness, which are for you, too.

Listen to His voice. Sing praises to Him. Sing songs aloud, all by yourself, as you work around the house or drive your car. His peace will flow like a river into and out from you, for you are His beloved child. Love Him. Trust Him.

Questions and Answers

QUESTION: How do you get Bible verses that guide you?

ANSWER: By reading your Bible daily, marking, and memorizing it. Notice how the Spirit leads, what people did, what they said, how they prayed, and how they obeyed.

QUESTION: Ros, do you ask the opinions of others?

ANSWER: Yes, I do, and share with them what is taking place.

QUESTION: What if they don't agree?

ANSWER: I search my heart again, and wait for the Lord again. I want to please Him, not people (John 10:3, 4). I love today's chorus that says, "They that wait upon the Lord shall renew their strength" (Isaiah 40:31).

Chapter Review

Here is a list of some of the ways God has guided people. Use this as a summary or review.

1. God speaks:
   through your reading these pages
   as you read the life stories of others
   as you read your Bible
   through surgery or illness
   through writing letters
   through sharing with another
   through a prayer partner
2. Show your trust in God's love by:
   making Christ first
   believing He has a plan for you
   being faithful just where you are
   waiting for the open door
   being willing to accept a change
   believing He will speak to you
3. What is the Lord saying to you through this chapter?

To us is given the privilege of walking in the light with Jesus, who is the light of the world, and we are promised that we shall not walk in darkness.

See John 8:12; Isaiah 50:10

8

Second Priority:
Your Life Partner

The success of your lifework and your happiness in life will in a large way be determined by your choice of a life partner. The reverse is also true. Your life partner may be one of the most important influences in your lifework.

Does the Lord God actually guide people regarding whom they should or should not marry? Is it His plan that every person born on this planet should have a mate? The answer to the first question is, yes. I'm no authority on the second (1 Corinthians 7:7, 8).

I do know that as children of God we are invited to give our whole selves to Him. Following Jesus is not something we do with part of ourselves. He has redeemed us—body, soul, and spirit—and He desires that His Spirit be active in every part of our lives. Nothing is our own to do with as we please.

As the branch lives in the vine and is a vital part of that vine it is supplied with all that is necessary for fruit bearing.

Pruning comes in order to cut away anything that will not contribute to its fruitfulness. Our purpose in this is to become like Jesus and to spread His love everywhere we go.

Since we are assured that Jesus' love is the love of the Father also, how can He be indifferent to our choices of loving and living? Again let us remind ourselves that we must submit our desires to Him and learn the lessons He teaches us through our disappointments and failures.

This chapter will explore how God leads us in the crucial matter of choosing a life partner or of living alone, including celibacy. Regardless of our marital status, God's basic standard is complete surrender to His holy will. What could be more fulfilling in this changeful, evil world, than being in the center of His will? If we settle for less, His faithfulness will guide us or discipline us until we cry out from deep within, "Lord, Thy will be done!"

Today's Marital Practices

In today's secular world, physical attraction seems to be the lodestar for getting married—or living together. How secure is that bond? How long does that last?

In the Old Testament it seems there was no problem in choosing a life partner—a husband or a wife. Parents usually chose husbands for their daughters, from their tribe or extended family. Such customs are still practiced in many parts of our world today.

Divorce sometimes is necessary, but God does heal marriages. I remember when I first became a staff member for Inter-Varsity, the divorce rate was one out of every four marriages. Today four out of every five end in divorce. Single parenting gets high visibility in women's magazines today.

If You Are Thinking of Getting Married

1. If your lifework is known, pray that God will prepare you for the person you will meet and marry, just as He is preparing that person.
2. Pray that you will meet the person He is choosing for you, one who will believe in you and assist you in your lifework.
3. You may even pray that such a person will have the same life calling.
4. Make it your aim to become good friends before you become lovers.
5. Do not marry an unbeliever. Marry a girl (or a guy) who loves Jesus as you do (2 Corinthians 6:14–16).

I suggest you talk to your Christian friends who are happily married or who have been divorced and remarried. They will give you advice that has been tested through the fires of suffering and heartbreak.

Don't settle for less when it comes to selecting a life partner. Pray that the Lord, who led you to a total surrender, will do the same for her or him. Learn to pray conversationally with each other. There is no better way to get to know each other in a deeper, intimate way.

The desire for a life partner is as firmly planted in every living person as is the heart that beats or the lungs that breathe. We are of the earth, earthy; yet we are spirit, with the breath of the living God in our nostrils and His Spirit in our hearts. Our sexuality is given to us for creative purposes that, when surrendered to the Lord, bring forth fruit in many directions; deep satisfaction results. This is true for both the single or the married person.

Only when we go our own way, not consulting the Lord God who made us, do we get into trouble and find ourselves in deep waters—with no seeming solution except divorce.

This happened to a young man I knew who was painfully hurt and disappointed when his marriage fell apart. If he had taken time to pray with her before marriage, it might have been a different story. Several days after the marriage vows had been said, when he suggested praying together, his young bride laughed in his face and asked him where in the world he ever got the idea that she would pray with him!

He had taken for granted that because her parents were devoted believers she was one, too. In fact, she used this young man as a cover-up, because she was already pregnant. That marriage ended in divorce, but eventually there was a happy ending for him.

After difficult, solitary years of finding himself and proving that Jesus Christ is sufficient, God led him to a young woman who had also gone through the heartbreak of divorce. Together they have a home dedicated to the will of God, to lifework in His will, and best of all a life partner sharing all this, because Jesus Christ is Lord of each of them.

I'll say it again, from my observation, the only foolproof way is to marry a person who loves the Lord Jesus as you do. Only the Spirit of God can direct you in this choice. The more mature you are, the more surrendered to your Lord, the easier it will be for you to hear and to obey His voice.

Learn to follow Jesus in everyday small things, and then when a big thing, like a life partner, comes along, you will have some good experience behind you. Set your priorities now in the will of God.

If You Are Unmarried

Whether or not you marry, there are some biblical priorities it would be well to have in mind before you even meet the "right person." Human emotions have a way of taking over and clouding every issue until after the knot is tied. The divorce rate is high, and who wants to be another negative statistic?

I can hear someone ask, "How can the subject of a life partner be one of God's priorities?" The times we live in seem to contradict the idea that there is a mate for each of us.

First of all, as a single person, God wants you to find the secret of being a whole person. That means you are not dominated by another, nor are you the domineering one. Avoid the mistake of getting married just to get away from home; that is jumping out of the frying pan into the fire.

Let Jesus Christ become the most important person in your life. Make His will your daily aim. His voice is speaking to you, and His Spirit will guide you, until every day is filled with fresh surprises.

Don't settle for anything less than God's choice when it

comes to selecting a life partner. If that partner is not forth-coming, get on your knees again and make a fresh surren-der. Wait for God's time and will. There is great freedom in doing the will of God, in obedience and holiness.

The gift of celibacy is given to some, and the power of temptation is taken care of by God's grace and power. The subject of celibacy and no life partner is coming up directly.

If Marriage Seems Improbable

What if marriage seems out of the question?
What about the person who sees the years going by and is still working and living alone?
What about the person who is prevented from marriage because of the care of an aged and invalid parent?
What about the person whose mother so dominates that marriage is impossible?
What about the divorced person who has small chil-dren to raise and needs to make a living?
What about a disabled person or a person serving a prison sentence?

Since our Lord Jesus assures us of His eternal love, the same love that the Father gives Him, how then can He be in-different to our need for security and love? This quality in our Lord convinced me that His gift of God-given love can be both given and received by both sexes without sinful in-volvement; that love brings creativity, peace, and compan-ionship into one's life.

Failure to surrender to God's will could mean you have

not considered the solitary life of Jesus Himself, or perhaps you are still suffering from loneliness and bitterness because of what life has already handed to you.

Obedience will give you strength for sacrificing your desires, your will, your plan and will open doors for loving fellowship with both single and married people.

Anyone who knows he belongs to Christ and abides in Him is meant to handle tensions and temptations.

> My grace is sufficient for you, for my power is made perfect in weakness.
>
> 2 Corinthians 12:9 RSV

If You Are Married

If you are married and know you are in the will of God, you may be interested in two helpful organizations conducting workshops for good marriages that could be even better: Christian Marriage Encounter and Marriage Enrichment. Your pastor can put you in touch with them.

Here are five positive jewels which they teach:

1. Lord, change me! I know that the Lord is in charge of my husband, and I cannot pretend that I am the Holy Spirit.
2. Once you are married, God honors that union. "Let no man put asunder. . . ."
3. Live in your marriage, believing that divorce is not an option.

4. God uses your spouse's weaknesses to strengthen you.
5. Your lifework could be your life partner, or your lifework could be your home and your family.

If you are married and know you are not in the will of God, remember that God can change people. I've heard many testimonies by spouses who have had prayers answered and marriages healed.

Be not unbelieving, my brother, my sister, but read your Bible. Take hold of the promises and stand on them. Heed the admonitions. Give the Lord what belongs to Him, love Him with your whole heart and soul. And ask, and keep asking that you may receive. Give thanks and keep giving thanks, that God will change both of you, so together you may love, serve, and praise Him.

Here is the word of the Lord that came to one troubled spouse: "God told me to love my husband, and He would change him."

Unhappy people know how to hide their feelings cleverly, but just the same, problems surface in physical ailments. Divorce is a cop-out in most cases, but facing up to what needs to be done requires a counselor who can help bring the couple to inner healing through Jesus Christ, who alone can heal old memories and give them a fresh start.

When your relationship with your life partner produces stress, incompatibility, and ulcers, your lifework suffers, too. To pursue your own way is to surely suffer the consequences of a broken heart or a broken marriage—or both.

God expects you to give your spouse or mate the same

kind of love He gives to you. His love persists in spite of your unfaithfulness to Him. He is committed to you and will never divorce you because your performance falls below His expectations. He loves each one of us for what we are and what we can become with His help. Our Lord Jesus on the cross sets the example for love and forgiveness.

Your acceptance of your spouse depends on your concept of God. Did you believe what you just read? Do you believe God is in charge of your life? of the life of your husband or wife? Then you must also believe that even your failures and weaknesses have a divine design in your lives. They are tools of God to help you trust Him.

Receive (not accept) your mate as God's gift made personally for you.

Only God can change people, and people are only changed in a climate of love and acceptance—the climate Jesus Christ brings to us, because He gave Himself for us, an offering and a sacrifice to God, as a fragrant aroma (Ephesians 5:2).

"Oh, my people, if you had only listened to Me . . ." is the message in the latter part of the book of Isaiah. Those who listen, those who have ears to hear, those who wait for the Lord's guidance and suffer the pain of honest confrontation find that life's fragile boat rights itself, and once more peace and harmony flourish.

We serve a risen Savior. There is nothing impossible with Jesus Christ. Ask, seek, and knock, for He stands there, waiting for you.

The Gift of Celibacy

Is celibacy the same as being unmarried or never getting married? No, it is not. Celibacy means a state of grace given by God to that person who surrenders his or her sexuality to Him and permits His Spirit to use all that creative energy according to His holy will (1 Corinthians 7:32–35).

Many of us in every denomination have been called to that extra mile. We have freely offered our sexuality to the Lord. Celibacy is a gift of the Spirit, and you will know when God has given it to you or called you into it (Matthew 19:12).

I speak to you as a single person, never having been married. Did I want marriage? Being a normal human being, I wanted a life partner, a home of my own, and children. It took me a long time to give up my own desires and accept God's gift (Philippians 3:7, 8).

Off and on again, I would surrender the whole subject of marriage, but the issue was never settled until I saw clearly that it involved the whole issue of sexuality, including love to God, love to others, and all the creative arts and gifts given to mankind.

My Own Story

Being, as it were, whisked away from others my own age when I went to China at age twenty, I found no eligible candidates there (even though I looked!). During one of my furloughs, the Lord began to show me what surrender really meant.

With a group of friends, I heard that veteran missionary Dr. E. Stanley Jones speak at the Hollywood Bowl. I'll never forget one thing he said: "You are not safe until you can stand the worst possible thing that could happen to you."

Actually my heart recoiled in fear, because the worst thing I could think of was, "What if I loved someone I could not have?"

In the passage of time what I feared did come to pass, more than once. Being a single person, I suppose all that story will never be told. But I lived through it all and came forth a wiser, more subdued, more loving and forgiving, even a more obedient disciple of Jesus.

All those experiences have had a direct bearing on the ministry God has given me through the years, through my books and my workshops and speaking engagements.

Here are the Scripture verses given to me:

> If you knew the gift of God, and who it is that is saying to you "Give me a drink," you would have asked him, and he would have given you living water. . . . Every one who drinks of this water [from Jacob's well] will thirst again, but whoever drinks of the water that I shall give him will never thirst; the water that I give him will become in him a spring of water welling up to eternal life.
>
> John 4:10, 13, 14 RSV

This bit of profound truth came to me through J. Hudson Taylor's life story. "Will never thirst" were the words my faith took hold of. *Will* means "it will come to pass." *Never* means what it says, "never." *Thirst* means "any unsatisfied need."

That resulted in a deep transformation. My dissatisfaction turned into a lifelong love affair with Jesus Christ, my Lord. I have learned, am still learning, what it means to love the Lord God with all my heart, with all my soul, with all my strength—and then, it follows, to love my neighbor as myself.

I dedicated my life to letting Jesus love others through me. He teaches me His ways, that I may teach others. I understand God must break me, prune me of selfishness, of lack of purpose, and discipline me because of ignorance of His ways.

Listening to the Reverend George A. Maloney, S. J., I know I am not the only one God teaches in this way. Father Maloney teaches that God purifies His children who surrender to Him, that He is constantly uprooting inordinate affection of self or others, for we cannot love God perfectly until we are purified, made holy and obedient.

I repeat, my life is dedicated to letting Jesus love others through me, to doing my best to know what it means to love another just as Jesus loves me, and to humbly repenting and asking forgiveness when I fail. Warm, lasting friendships that stretch the soul and bring quiet joy can be made with both brothers and sisters in the Lord.

> . . . we are able to hold our heads high no matter what happens and know that all is well, for we know how dearly God loves us, and we feel this warm love everywhere within us because God has

given us the Holy Spirit to fill our hearts with his love.

Romans 5:5 TLB

Chapter Review

Under the following headings, write down a few of the guidelines given in this chapter to help you hear and obey the voice of the Lord.

1. If you are thinking of getting married:

2. If you are unmarried:

3. If marriage seems improbable:

4. If you are married:

5. If God has given you the gift of celibacy:

9

Third Priority:
Your Use of Money

Does God care what I do with my money? Apparently He does, for it is written many times, in the Old and New Testaments, that tithes and offerings belong to the Lord and are to be given to those who are called to do special work as priests and servants of the Most High God.

Thinking about money and God speaking to us about it, the thought came: *How can God speak about any subject if I am perfectly content with my own way of doing things?* The only answer I know is to turn back to the Chapter Review in chapter 6 and read that entire list until some item strikes you—makes you stop and think—and the Holy Spirit whispers, "Why not ask Me? Let Me guide you."

What you and I do with our money depends on a number of things: what our parents did or did not teach us, our ability to save or spend or to live on what we make, and our willingness to obey the Lord.

If you are one of those to whom the gift of making money has been given, then your responsibility to the Lord God is greater than the blue-collar man who takes home a check every two weeks, which must last until the next payday.

Our dearest treasure, whatever or whoever it may be, has been given to us by the Great Giver of Life, in trust, as it were. We who follow Jesus know that all must eventually be relinquished into His hands, in fact, gladly given back to Him—not really ours anymore.

God is speaking to each of us right now, while we are reading this, of how much He loves us, of the good things in life that He has given us, of the failures He has redeemed, of the plans He has for us as we walk in the light with Him.

> If you want to know what God wants you to do, ask him, and he will gladly tell you, for he is always ready to give a bountiful supply of wisdom to all who ask him. . . . But . . . be sure that you really expect him to tell you. . . .
>
> James 1:5, 6 TLB

Jesus mentioned money (in His teachings and parables) more than any other subject, for stewardship of a person's money is measured by his ability to think clearly and follow through when it comes to handling it. I'm grateful for the Scripture teaching given to me as a teenager in our little church.

First Lessons in Tithing

Immediately upon entering the new life with Christ, at the age of fifteen, I learned that ten cents out of every dollar I earned (or was given to me) belonged to God.

Strange, isn't it, I can hardly remember anything before the age of fifteen, for life really began for me then. Perhaps because I gave it to Jesus, and it was His to do with as He pleased, not mine any longer.

I watched my elders follow the scriptural teaching. Their tithes went into the Sunday offering plate, and so did mine.

From that time until now, every cent of money coming into my hands has been carefully tithed, and in later years sometimes doubled or tripled. I have never borrowed money or been in debt. The little I had has always been sufficient.

The Day of Reckoning

So carefully did I tithe in those early years that I noted it in a small notebook in my purse. One side listed what came in, and the other side what belonged to God and where it went.

I actually felt proud of those sheets, because doing what God wanted me to do with my money gave me a sense of values, of pride, of joy, of discipline, which affected the rest of my life.

Then the day of reckoning came. My salary as a young missionary-secretary in a China mission was very small, but what belonged to God was carefully given. I don't recall the

catalyst, but I do remember that I was brought face-to-face
with the fact that I had only given God what belonged to
Him. I had never given Him one, single offering to show my
thanks or my gratitude or my love. Why, I had actually
withheld from Him!

You might say I acted stingily, selfishly, only following
the letter of the law because it was expected of me. No love
gifts to the One who loved me most!

I knew the Lord was speaking to me, and I prayed for
wisdom to know what to do. The answer came. "All your
tithe has been put into China so far; why not have a part in
My church in India?" Soon God led me to start supporting
an orphan in India and, since then, also in other countries.

I should tell you that I was truly grieved in my heart and
open for more instruction. What else should I do? Where
else could I give? Looking around at my blessings, I saw
clothing and shoes in my closet, which I was not wearing.

"Give them away," came the instruction from within. I
did, sharing with others who had less. But God had much
more to show me. It still had to do with the particular clothing I was wearing.

At that particular time, I was a member of a team of
young women from the Oriental Missionary Society's Bible
Institute, in Peking. We traveled from one rural village to
another, teaching and helping the local pastors. Suddenly I
saw what I possessed: so much more than any of the people I
taught, even more than any of the young women in my
Team. I had three fur-lined *cheong shams* (coats)! I had a
long-haired sheepskin one, with the fur inside, for warmth,

to wear in rural areas; over this I wore a plain blue cloth one, for protection. Then, because I needed warmth when I got back into the city (and the sheepskin one needed cleaning to be ready for the next trip), I finally bought a nice fox fur (hundreds of pieces from the side of the foxes' heads, sewed together) with a lovely blue silk exterior. I loved that one; it was so light and warm, and I felt elegant when I wore it. Finally (would my needs ever stop?), because I did not want to wear Chinese clothes to the American, English-speaking church, I had to get another fur coat. A nice, soft rabbit-skin lining for a black cloth coat. All these were made by expert Chinese tailors. Now I felt ready for any place, any weather, any time. Looking at those three fur-lined garments, I saw how much more I had than the people I came to love and serve. They were lucky to own one cotton padded garment. Dear Lord, what should I do? Where should I start?

The words from Malachi 3:8–10 (TLB) came to my attention:

> "Will a man rob God? Surely not! And yet you have robbed me."
>
> "What do you mean? When did we ever rob you?"
>
> "You have robbed me of the tithes and offerings due to me. . . ."
>
> [Then the curse is written for those who refuse and the blessing for those who obey.]
>
> "Try it! Let me prove it to you."

There it was. I had carefully, miserly, given to the Lord exactly one-tenth of all the money that had ever come into my hands.

But where were the offerings? When had I ever given a love offering to my Lord? The answer: never.

My repentance and grief surely came from the Holy Spirit, who convicts of sin, the sin of withholding from the Lord God that which is His, not mine. *Why, everything I have comes from Him!* I reminded myself, with more tears and more repentance.

A broken heart is of great value in the sight of the Lord. I wanted to know where to start, and I received a clear answer. "Those three fur-lined garments ... how much did they cost? Total the amount, then give as I direct, until it is balanced."

Love Offerings to My Lord

I was amazed at what began to happen after that.

Our gateman, a wizened old man who carefully inspected everyone who wanted to come into our compound (which consisted of homes, church, and seminary, surrounded by a wall), guarded the only entrance.

One day he approached me as I was about to leave on an errand. Old Wong Lau-tai-tai couldn't attend church anymore, because her son stole her only pair of "lily-shoes," right off her feet while she was sleeping, to buy opium for himself. That meant she had bound feet, yet she walked to church. God knows how far! But another opportunity for me. The gateman sent me to one of our pastors, and I put a sum into his hands, which eventually became a new pair of "lily-shoes" for old Mrs. Wong.

Maybe you guessed what I did. Yes, I started a new page with the total figure of the three fur-lined garments and began to list amounts given away on the other side, just to be sure. And you can be certain I went over the top, too. It turned out to be fun and exciting, just seeing where the next opportunity would be given.

Again the gateman told me. At the women's meeting held in the street chapel that day, a teenager had been found quietly weeping her heart out. She had been sold by her father, ran away, and was now homeless, hungry, tired, disheveled, and desperate.

Hai-ming was invited to come to my little Chinese apartment, made from four storerooms along the inside of the great wall surrounding our compound. My serving maid gave her a bath and washed her hair; the girls in the dormitory donated clothes. A hot meal and a good night's rest helped. Then we could talk to her about the true God who loved her. She lived with me for several years while she went to school, and more figures were written off my page of special offerings.

The Lord not only taught me to listen to Him about the use of my money; He also taught me what it meant to love my neighbor as myself. That it was pleasing to Him, when I not only gave myself, but my home and my money to help His children. I learned that Scripture taught that the tithe should go to your church or those actively in the service of the Lord, but that offerings could go to His needy children wherever He directed.

What About Borrowing and Lending?

This was the next subject the Lord began to talk to me about, when it came to money.

"Lord, speak to me. Are You pleased if I borrow money?"

"My child, why not trust Me to supply your needs."

> . . . My God shall supply all your need according to his riches in glory by Christ Jesus.
>
> Philippians 4:19

I had twice trusted my Lord to supply the steamer fare to China. I trusted Him to raise up faithful friends and prayer partners to give support while I was in China. Why now would I want to put myself in hock to another human being and owe something? Why not trust my Lord to supply in His way and His time and quietly do without and wait until He did.

Then the Lord spoke to me through one of our seminary students. Chan knocked on my door one afternoon. I poured him a cup of tea, and we exchanged polite conversation. He finally came to the point: The check from his father had not come for three months. He had a bad toothache, and the dentist demanded cash; would I lend him ten dollars?

I would, and I did. But I failed to reckon with what would happen afterward. As the weeks passed and grew into months, Chan avoided me on all occasions, if possible. I grew uneasy, knowing how little most of our students lived on and how they really did trust the Lord to supply their needs.

What had I done? I had laid a load of guilt on him because he could not repay me. I had cut off fellowship with my brother in Christ.

What was wrong? I took the whole subject to Jesus and prayed about it. Scripture I had previously memorized flashed into mind (which I knew was the faithfulness of the Holy Spirit reminding me of what I already knew).

> Give, and it shall be given unto you; good measure, pressed down, and shaken together, and running over, shall men give into your bosom. For with the same measure that ye mete withal it shall be measured to you again.
>
> Luke 6:38

There was my answer. Next time anyone asked to borrow money, first pray with him and show him Scriptures in Luke and Philippians and then tell him I would give him X number of dollars as a gift—no debt, no repaying. Assure him that the Lord will supply his need, even as mine has been supplied.

I spoke to Chan, assuring him that the old debt was canceled, that instead he was to consider the loan a free gift from the Lord and to give thanks.

My own heart overflowed with thanks to God. He spoke, and I heard His instructions. I had learned another lesson in giving and, best of all, a way to assist someone and simultaneously make friends instead of enemies.

Sequel to Those Lessons

With the constant guidance given by the Holy Spirit, many times in spite of my own ignorance, I have enjoyed a rich spate of years giving to others and increasing my giving. I've watched the Lord give back to me through others. I followed His instructions for about thirty years, and then I failed to follow through on what He had taught me.

I lent money, instead of giving it, to a dear and valued friend who was unable to manage payments on her home and who might otherwise have lost it. When the Lord spoke and reminded me I was to give, not to lend, I wrote off the amount as a gift, for I didn't want to lose that friendship, nor did I want to risk disobeying Jesus. People we lend to tend to trust us, instead of the Lord God Himself.

Scriptural Teaching

Does God care about what we do with our money? Does He care where we give tithes and offerings? Yes, God does care. It began with Abraham, a long time ago, when he gave the priest, Melchizedek, a tithe of all the loot he took from his enemies. Genesis 14:20 records this, and Hebrews 7 goes into that same subject, with the same requirement laid upon us in this present age: One-tenth of all we own belongs to the Lord from whom it came in the first place. He will guide us, and He will speak to us about where our offerings can best accomplish His purposes.

"Will a man rob God?" The Prophet Malachi asked this question, and the Lord answered: "And yet you have robbed me of the tithes and offerings due to me."

Martha and John Prove the Promise

My former secretary and good friend, Martha, told me that when she married John, he thought twenty-five cents dropped in the plate was enough. She was able to convince him to try tithing. At first to give 10 percent of the $108.00 he brought home seemed like a terrible amount.

"But we've proven the Lord's promise that He will pour out blessings we cannot contain. Once, when one of the boys was small, we just couldn't give the tithe and pay the doctor, too, but we decided that the Lord came first. Believe it or not, the rest stretched farther than ever.

"John believes in giving off the top. He says the government wants taxes from the gross, so why shouldn't God have the tithe from the gross and not the net?

"When my sister-in-law thought it was terrible that we gave ten dollars a week (many years ago), I finally said to her, 'We don't give the church as much as you and your husband spend on booze and cigarettes!' "

Moral of that story: You can never get in debt to God. Today Martha and John have a thriving custom upholstery business and are receiving God's blessing in their business, their church, their children and grandchildren.

Questions and Answers

QUESTION: What about family problems when there is an inheritance to be divided?

ANSWER: I'm sure our Lord is grieved over the competition, jealousy, and unfair means some family members stoop to. Prevention is the best answer; in other words, make a fair will and be sure it is brought up-to-date every few years.

QUESTION: Can one give the tithe to family, to the elderly needing help?

ANSWER: Personally, I do not believe the Bible teaches this. When you give your tithe to the Lord's work He will make the rest go farther, and your needs will be met.

QUESTION: What is "storehouse tithing"?

ANSWER: Some denominations interpret this as the Bible principle of bringing all of one's tithe into the local church. Often great pressure is brought upon individuals who give part of their tithe somewhere else (to others serving the Lord). In the Old Testament there was only one Tabernacle, then only one Temple, only one priestly tribe of Levi. Today's religious pattern is very different. One needs to pray, to listen to the voice of the Lord, and give as He directs (not to the multitude of requests that fill one's mailbox). It is usually the small donations that keep the Lord's work going, not the large ones.

QUESTION: What if I have no money to give, and my husband will not share my views?

ANSWER: One lady I know tithes the grocery money her husband gives her. I remember my own parents, struggling to make ends meet with six children to raise. While she and Dad had very little to give, Mother talked about tithing to every unmarried person who ever came into our home! Foreign missions were the love of her heart, and through her hands, more than $8,000.00 went to missionaries, because of her vision. It all came from those employed single people to whom she spoke. Now that I think about it, I'm sure Mother heard the voice of the Lord in all her everyday life.

QUESTION: Is it wrong to borrow money for a car, for a house, or for a business loan?

ANSWER: That depends.

1. The answer is yes, it is wrong, if in the past you have been unable to meet your obligations. Financing and credit come so easily today that we overextend ourselves, and the first thing we cut is our tithes and offerings. Then we are in for more trouble.

2. The answer is no, it's not wrong, if you have talked to the Lord and some re-

sponsible person about your plans. Sometimes another can think more clearly and more objectively. Give your plans to the Lord, along with your car, your house, your business, and be His steward to manage them. If your economic future is fairly secure and you know God is leading you—might sound like a contradiction, but the Holy Spirit will give you an inner conviction.

3. Otherwise, how about doing without until God speaks? or better still, until He provides what He has had in mind for you all along, which could be something very different from what you had in mind.

Chapter Review

1. What has the Lord said to you during the reading of chapter 9? It's important that you share it with someone.
2. The Lord will speak to you through His Word from 2 Corinthians 8–10. I recommend *The Living Bible* for a fresh and startling confrontation.

Basic Principles in Giving

The following outline is taken from chapters 8–10 of Paul's second letter to the Corinthians. Read the verses.

Pray over them. Ask the Lord what He wants to say to you about your money. Then count the cost of giving Him everything, but especially tithes and offerings.

1. Joy and sometimes poverty will overflow when you give to others (8:2).
2. Give more than you can afford and be enthusiastic (8:3).
3. Share what God has given to you with the leaders who teach you. God will direct you (8:5).
4. Be a leader in cheerful giving (8:7).
5. Giving proves your love is real (8:8).
6. Look at Jesus' example. "For you know the grace of our Lord Jesus Christ, that though he was rich, yet for your sake he became poor, so that by his poverty you might become rich" (2 Corinthians 8:9 RSV).
7. Give from what you have, not from what you do not have (8:12).
8. Divide with others, since you have plenty; later they can help you in the same way (8:14).
9. Don't force another to give (9:7).
10. Give joyfully, trust God for your own needs (9:8).

Results

Praise is given to God.
Those whom you have helped will give God praise.
They will pray for you.
And you will love one another.

Part III

How Do We Tune In?

Now we are at the crucial part of your reading, which will reveal the inner intentions of your heart. How ready and willing are you to forsake all, including yourself, and follow Jesus?

No progress, no new venture, no new step is ever taken without a definite decision. The invitation, the drawing power of love, plus the future plans are all initiated by our loving Father. He is ready to give every good thing to enable you to obey His Voice and carry out His will. The power is His, but He needs you and me to step out in faith and trust Him. Make your decision. Trust Him.

> His mother said to the servants: "Do whatever he tells you."
>
> John 2:5 RSV

> ... A servant is not greater than his master. ...
>
> John 13:16 RSV

"No longer do I call you servants, for the servant does not know what his master is doing; but I have called you friends, for all that I have heard from my Father I have made known to you. You did not choose me, but I chose you and appointed you that you should go and bear fruit and that your fruit should abide; so that whatever you ask the Father in my name, he may give it to you."

John 15:15, 16 RSV

10

By the Risk of Obedience

I will instruct thee and teach thee in the way
which thou shalt go: I will guide thee with mine
eye.

Psalms 32:8

If anyone loves me, he will obey my teaching.
My Father will love him, and we will come to him
and make our home with him.

John 14:23 NIV

How can one know the teaching of Jesus unless he reads
the Bible carefully, marks and memorizes it, and thus hides
it away in his heart? Almost as important, his ears must be
opened to hear what the Lord God is saying to him regarding every aspect of his life.

Love wants to be near the loved one. Jesus and His Father
promise to live with, make their home with, the one who
loves Him—and let's not forget the other word—obeys Him.

Question: Does love always obey the lover? Is not love

119

sometimes very selfish and grasping and adept at ignoring another? Answer: The love spoken of by Jesus is not the variegated human kind, but the special Holy Spirit kind of love, rooted in the eternal unconditional love of God.

To know more about this love of God in our hearts, read Romans 8; 1 Corinthians 13; and Philippians 1:9–11, which is Paul's prayer that pure love might result in depth of insight and spiritual knowledge.

Obedience Versus Love

I purposely started this chapter with love as a necessary catalyst for obedience, because that word *obedience* has been a block, a hindrance, an unwanted word all my life. Only recently has the subject of obedience appeared in my writings. Even my friends were not aware of this. And only recently have I been able to look at it objectively and find the source. Healing of memories somehow never got to that word! But Jesus in His faithfulness did. Praise Him!

My previous books are full of the love of God and the love of Jesus and the love of the Spirit. I know now that love was the missing factor in my own early life; obedience dominated.

God gave me two wonderful parents, who loved Him, each other, and their children. Being the eldest of six, the big sister, I constantly cared for the younger ones. Mother and Dad provided for us, gave us good training, and loved us in their own way, I'm sure. But I can't remember either of them ever telling me I was loved or hugging me. My father was easygoing, but my mother acted like a majordomo. She was devoted to her Lord, and she did her best to bring us up right. She kept all six of us busy, and her word was law; we all went through the spanking era, even to cutting the willow switches in the backyard and lying over the kitchen chair!

Any disobedience was carefully hidden away, and we seldom told on each other. Obedience was a bad word. However, we all turned out pretty well.

The church I belonged to emphasized "holiness unto the Lord" and "separation from sin and sinners." This of course meant in our dress, our hair, our cosmetics, our jewelry (too bad if you were born a female, eh?), as well as in our recreation, with always more emphasis put on what we did not do than what we did do. If they emphasized the latter, it concerned whether or not we had sinned.

As I look back on that negative pattern of life and remember how long it took me to really believe that our Lord was not a negative God, I marvel that I fell for it. I expect a kind of brainwashing had taken place, and God forgive me if I am judging harshly.

Under the ruse of obedience and being holy to the Lord, as a teenager I looked different than my classmates. They wore bobby socks, cut their hair, and wore lipstick. I wore long, black stockings, had long hair and no lipstick. No movies, either, but today all the old ones are on TV, and you can see them in your own home. But mind you, I was being "obedient to the Lord and being separate."

Perhaps all of that had something to do with my delight as an adult in finally discovering the Episcopal Church, which did not demand this outward conformity. Only the blessedness of weekly Eucharist (Lord's Supper), with audience participation that made me feel and be part of the Body of Christ. Thanks be to God for leading me to Saint James Church, where we experience the renewal in full swing and glorify the Lord through the praises of His people.

All the above adds up to one statement: The inner love and obedience of God's child is more important than the outward appearance.

Now what about you, my reader? Where is the emphasis in your Christian life? on love or obedience? or partial truth, including one or the other? On human interpretation or inner conviction given by the Holy Spirit?

God loves you unconditionally, and His love depends not on what you do or don't do. He loves you because it is His nature to love.

All my life has been a pilgrimage in loving Jesus, in knowing He loved me, and in wanting to do what He told me to do, because ours is a love relationship. As time went by that love began to overflow into my books, my ministry, and to people around me.

The word *obedience* had a harsh and unpleasant connotation, and I avoided it. I can see now that I acted out that obedience in spirit, even if I shied away from the word. I substituted other words: hearing the Lord speak to me, doing His will. You see, if I emphasized obeying the Lord and then failed to obey Him, it might mean Jesus and His Father would not continually remain in my heart. That is how I interpreted John 14:21, 23.

Such rationalization has become a thing of the past, thank

God. I know now that I am His forever and that He forgives me, cleanses me, speaks to me, guides me, redeems my failures, and nothing in this world or the next can separate me from His love (Romans 8:31–39).

Yes, obedience involves a risk. Did I really hear God speaking to me? Does that Bible verse mean what I think it means? What will other people think? What if I am hearing the wrong voice?

The answers to those questions have already been dealt with in the first chapters of this book. My heart is full of praise for the faithfulness of the blessed Holy Spirit, who will not allow my spirit to rest when He wants to tell me something or He has a task for me. Such an instance occurred about three years ago, but as yet I am not at liberty to share it. Great freedom and blessing has come because I obeyed the Lord in spite of the risk of that obedience. It was worth it.

In the remainder of this chapter I want to briefly share some of the risks other people took when they obeyed the Lord and heard His voice speak to them.

These Took a Risk for Jesus' Sake

George. This is a true story about a brother whom we shall call George. A member of an Episcopal Church, he attended a Life in the Spirit class and received the baptism of the Spirit. This alerted him to the voice of the Lord, the leading of the Spirit, and to the gifts the Spirit gives God's people for the upbuilding of His Body.

"Lord, what do You want me to do? I'm retired, and I don't seem to have any gifts to help anybody. Speak to me, tell me what to do."

The answer that came George couldn't believe! "Go to the parish kitchen, get a pail of water, and scrub that floor."

George couldn't believe it! Why was God saying that to him? He asked again and again, and each time the same instruction came through. What would people think? With all his years of business experience, wasn't there something else God had for him to do?

Finally George gave in. He hoped no one would be in the parish hall that day. He got down on his hands and knees and gave that floor a good, hard scrubbing. Nobody came. And George received the blessing of having obeyed His Lord.

Some time went by, and once more George asked for guidance. Once more the same instruction came. This time he had fewer excuses, but somebody saw him.

"Why, George, what in the world are you doing down there?"

George sat back on his knees, "I'm obeying the Lord. He told me to do this, and I'm doing it."

The word got around that George (former president of the bank, senior warden of the vestry) heard God speaking to him! That he actually scrubbed the kitchen floor because God spoke to him!

Quietly a new ministry began for George, as one man after another from that church came to him for help in knowing how to hear the voice of the Lord. God knew what

He was doing. When we humble ourselves before the Lord, He will lift us up in His own time.

The Unnamed Woman of Faith (Mark 5:25–34).   I love this story of the woman who touched Jesus' garment. While the main teaching focuses on healing through faith, it includes an extra bonus that escapes many readers.

Let's look at the risk of obedience that possessed her so that she had to touch Jesus.

> 1. What if she were not healed? Her inner convictions overcame this doubt, for it was her last hope. She had already endured twelve years of illness (hemorrhaging) and suffered under many physicians.
>
> 2. What if someone recognized her? According to Jewish law, anyone who touched her (in her condition) was defiled, and cleansing took a week of purification.
>
> 3. Then she faced the unknown risk of what might happen, and it did happen. There was fear, humiliation, and confession as she fell at His feet.

Now comes the unexpected blessing of obedience: Jesus spoke to her. He lifted her up and called her daughter. She was given what all of us so desire and long for. She heard His voice. She saw His face. I'm sure praise and thanksgiving filled her heart for many months to come.

The risk of obedience was worth it.

Ken and Gloria Copeland.   In her book *God's Will for You* Gloria Copeland writes an introduction that is worth the price of the book. The risk of obedience this young couple took again and again to follow the will of the Lord led them through some difficult times. But through TV and national programs today we all know how greatly God gifted them and is using them for the upbuilding of His people.

Ken was a commercial pilot and ex nightclub singer when they got married. They experienced dire circumstances as he went from one job to another. Then through a New Testament given to them by his praying mother, they read Matthew 6:25–34.

> But seek ye first the kingdom of God . . . and all these things shall be added unto you.
>
> Matthew 6:33

Jesus Christ moved into their hearts, and they continued to read. In two weeks Ken had a new job and soon a new car, a new apartment, and new furniture. Three months later they received the Holy Spirit, and Ken was called into the ministry.

Then God guided them to Oral Roberts University, where, because of low finances as students, they learned to trust God. Ken was assigned to Oral Roberts' airplane as copilot, which meant he was present at many great healing services.

The story of Ken and Gloria Copeland is the story of a man and woman who risked obedience to follow the Lord. They trusted His Word (Philippians 4:19) and His Presence with them. In closing, Gloria writes, the story of their life is

"... what God's Word will do in your life if you will obey Him."

Ruth Carter Stapleton. When Ruth Stapleton was in California a few years ago, I heard her tell the story of how God led her into her present ministry.

After she felt the call in her heart to teach Inner Healing, God tested her through some humbling circumstances, until she finally was ready for His open door.

Sharing God's call with the elders of the church, they gave her an assignment: working in the church kitchen! She was disappointed and felt put down, but after praying about it, decided that even though she had no talents along that line, she would do her best. The next move: into the dining room, to set up and decorate tables. After that: into the nursery, taking care of little ones.

> Although he was a Son, he learned obedience through what he suffered.
>
>   Hebrews 5:8 RSV

Finally the door opened. She had been faithful in smaller matters, now in the larger matter of teaching Inner Healing, she was given prayer support and a wide-open door, which eventually led her all over the world and to author several books on that subject.

Madame Bilquis Sheik. The first time I heard Madame Sheik was at one of the huge services in the Shrine Auditorium, held by Kathryn Kuhlman, in Los Angeles. Madame was not only a striking figure in her silver sari, but her deep voice and beautiful English demanded our attention as we heard her unusual testimony.

Madame was born into a long generation of wealthy rulers in Pakistan, but estrangement from her husband and living alone in luxury brought a longing to know more than the Koran taught.

At great risk she obtained a Bible, and while reading it in a hospital, a little nun asked why she didn't pray to the God she was searching for. "Talk to Him as if He were your Father."

Because she dared to call God Father and to follow Jesus, she faced more risks and persecution than I can tell you here. With no teacher except the Holy Spirit, her life underwent a complete change: attitudes, values, ideas, reactions and alibis—no more white lies, only truth. The Bible must be lived, not merely read; it must be understood and obeyed. Saying "Lord, Lord" is not enough.

She braved the isolation threatened and imposed by her family; she visited "foreign" missionaries; she invited village children into her fruit garden once a week; she even held a fellowship meeting in her home for any believers who wished to attend. Through trial and error, God taught her, until finally her new faith cost her not only the loss of her home, but exile in a strange land, America.

Her message to us is the one God gave to her: *Seek My Presence, not results.*

Chapter Review

1. Memorize the two verses at the beginning of this chapter. Write them on a card or piece of paper and put them in your pocket. God speaks as you memorize and meditate.
2. When was the last time you obeyed the word of the Lord? Share it with someone as a love gift to your Lord.
3. Is there any major part of your life about which the Lord is speaking? Say yes, and you will receive power to start obeying Him.
4. Examine carefully the things you can or can't do and search your heart to determine if you are obeying man or God (Ephesians 6:5–8; Mark 7:14–23; 1 Peter 4:14, 15).

11

By My Commitment to Jesus Christ

In the final two chapters, we will open our hearts first to the need for a deeper personal commitment in order to hear God speaking clearly and then to the need for understanding and receiving the fullness of the Holy Spirit. He helps us in all our weakness and gives us ability to listen and power to carry out the will of God to the glory of Christ our Lord.

C. S. Lewis once wrote that God whispers to us in our pleasures, speaks to us in our conscience, but shouts in our pains, trying to rouse a deaf world to hear His voice.

Why must God shout at us to get our attention? Why must pain, heartbreak, surgery, or loss of a loved one get us quiet long enough for Him to get our complete attention?

Briefly: we become too busy—too busy with our pleasures, with the demands upon our time, until pain hits us. We seem unable to keep our priorities straight. Something has to give, so the quiet, contemplative devotional times go

130

by the board, until we are brought up with a shock, that God is wanting our attention.

When did God last speak to you? Was it a small or a big thing? Did you share it with anyone? How many of your close friends share with you what the Lord tells them? Are we afraid of each other? Are we such private persons? Or have we been hurt too many times?

Three Hindrances to Commitment

One of the magazines I receive is *New Covenant,* a Catholic charismatic monthly. The September 1983 issue reports on a message given by Sister Ann Therese Shields when she spoke to 170 prayer group leaders. She commented on several prophecies she had recently heard; all of them spoke of the ways God's power can actually be blocked by the following:

1. Fear of surrendering oneself to God.
2. Compromises with sin and the spirit of the world.
3. A lack of commitment to holiness.

To me personal commitment means: loving the Lord God with all my heart, with all my mind, with all my soul, with all my strength, and my neighbor as myself.

Personal commitment means giving away all right to myself, body, soul, and spirit to Jesus Christ. It means "others may, but I cannot." It means a thankful spirit (and mouth) for all my Lord provides as well as withholds. It means ears ready to hear and carry out any message He gives me.

Personal commitment also means willingness to admit when I fail, grace to repent and confess, and more grace to get up and go on. That takes care of any compromise with sin or any spirit of worldliness. The hardest part comes when others do not understand or are unwilling to accept my apology as sincere. That means leaving my reputation in God's hands.

The third commitment to holiness will be discussed in the next chapter. Holiness depends on the Holy Spirit, who imparts it.

God Gets Our Attention

In my own daily devotions I've been reading the book of Ezekiel in *The Living Bible,* because the English is simpler. I find it very depressing to read the judgments Jehovah God spoke against His people in chapter after chapter. The reason for the wars, the slain, the spoiling of property, and even the destruction of Jerusalem and the Temple, was because His people turned to worship idols instead of the One True God to whom they belonged.

In our world today, most of us have our own personal, political or religious "gods," which take our attention from the One True God who redeemed us and made us His own, even going so far as to call us the Bride of Christ.

I'm not speaking of those outside the church. I'm speaking to those of us who are named by His name. Let us examine our commitment to love and to serve the One True God.

Who is to name your fears or mine? What will happen if we make a total commitment to Jesus Christ? Who will condemn us for slipping into the ways of the world around us, which take our attention from our Lord? When will we recognize these gods, repent of them, and once again yield ourselves to total commitment to our Lord who yearns over us, loves us, and waits for us, who even permits calamity to descend upon us in order to get our attention?

God's methods of getting our attention seldom meet with our approval, but speak He does, and speak He will. The difference is in how we hear Him—in how we accept those hurts and heartbreaks He permits life to hand us and how we make the choices that confront us.

If anyone wants to get my attention, he can make a telephone call, write a personal letter, or come and visit me. In any case, my answer is forthcoming. Can I do less when Jesus uses a variety of means to get my attention?

God got Moses' attention and spoke to him, but not until Moses *stopped*—turned aside to watch that bush burn—then the voice came to him. Just so, when we cease what we are doing and listen and wait, then the message will come to us also.

You might follow through on Moses, on his unwillingness to go alone, his need for a partner, his professed inability to speak, and so on. Each objection was met by the Lord God, until Moses had no more words. He surrendered and obeyed. God's persistence won. He always wins. When God calls, no escape exists.

Jesus Called His Disciples

He called them to total commitment: to leave everything behind, to follow Him and learn from Him. However, they were actually unable to put anything into practice until after the coming of the Holy Spirit at Pentecost. Until then, they lacked power.

Of His own total commitment, our Lord said a few things that time after time bring a kind of terror to me as I realize what the "now" step will cost me.

> . . . Unless a grain of wheat falls into the earth and dies, it remains alone; but if it dies, it bears much fruit. He who loves his life loses it, and he who hates his life in this world will keep it for eternal life. If any one serves me, he must follow me; and where I am, there shall my servant be also; if any one serves me, the Father will honor him.
>
> John 12:24–26 RSV

Jesus Invites You: "Follow Me"

Our religious vocabulary is filled with words we take for granted. For instance, Jesus just invited us: "Follow me, and where I am there shall my servant be."

We all pray: "Lord, speak to me."

He has already spoken. He spoke in the above verses, and He speaks in the verses you read daily. He speaks in the Scripture you hear read in worship on Sunday mornings. Now it's our turn to speak to Him, clause by clause, using the thoughts found in the above verses.

> Lord, I'm partially willing to be that grain of wheat. Make me entirely willing. I want to be willing.

I dread the dark of being alone.
Of dying alone in the dark.
I like the life I'm living, and I want more.
You ask me to want less?
You ask me to lose my life?
By turning my back on myself?
By hating myself, as it were?
You invite me to follow You if I would serve You,
To be where You are, not anywhere else.
Have mercy on me and assist me.
I want to serve You, to follow You only.
I want to start—now.
Now and forever. Amen.

Preparing, writing, and praying that prayer of surrender, that emptying prayer, brings back several times in my life when it seemed God asked the ultimate from me. I will not go into detail here, maybe sometime if I write the story of my life (to be published posthumously!).

When the call of God came to leave the missionary office and go into China's villages to preach the Gospel, it meant a break with the mission I belonged to. Where would I go? How would I be supported? I was willing, and God made a way.

Again the word of the Lord came for me to leave the comfortable American-style home we missionaries lived in and make a couple of storerooms along the wall into my own little Chinese apartment. I lived there several years with God's blessing.

Then the word of the Lord came to me to sell all I had and

follow Him. I had only a few possessions. I shed some tears of farewell in letting them go, but I did it, and He guided me into the next step.

Finally the word of the Lord came (after two years of putting it off) to accept invitations from a despised group of people who asked for my teaching. I tested that word, accepted it, and all the results are in God's hands, not mine.

When you read these pages, I'll be close to the eighty mark. What else can the Lord ask of me? One thing I'm sure of: the unconditional love of Jesus for me, which possesses my heart—that message must be passed on to others.

Have I failed to hear His word? Oh, yes, I'm sure I have. The good news is: Jesus redeems all our failures! Praise Him!

This month, in my own church, Saint James Episcopal, Newport Beach, I teach a six-week class on the subject of this book. Today, after church service, someone asked me if my teaching would be from the new book. I replied, "I'll be teaching from the manuscript, yes, but I'll be adding things I couldn't put on paper. It's one thing to share by word of mouth, and it's another to put it into print, where people misunderstand and judge." My friend agreed.

To Follow Jesus

To follow Jesus and become a grain of wheat, dying to one's own way, is not a momentary thing. It goes on year after year, as through both humiliating failure and heart obedience, we are taught more of our Lord's grace of forgiveness and His unconditional love.

To follow Jesus and give up all to Him means being willing to reread all His teachings and follow through, step by step, in daily life as the Spirit guides us and speaks to us.

To follow Jesus means to go where He sends you, to do what He asks you (without trying to save yourself), because ours is a love relationship, not because we want to be "used" by Him, but because we want to be where He is. To follow Jesus means to live in the light with Him, where there is no part dark, and to keep living in that light. To follow Jesus means to put away whatever smells like sin or worldliness (which draws me away from Him) and present myself, like a clay pot, to be cleansed and ready for His purposes.

The Meaning of Personal Commitment

Personal commitment is necessary for any disciple of Christ, not only for religious or ordained or "full-time" servants of God. All of us must know His voice when He speaks and willingly follow His guidance. That means anything He may ask, regarding our past, our present, or our future.

My mother taught me, as a teenager, that saying yes to the Lord Jesus was like two baskets. One basket contained all I knew then, and I could put a great big yes on it. The other basket was covered and contained the unknown future; I could put a whole lot of yeses on that one, to be used when the time came.

Actually, full commitment means counting the cost in specific details such as: life partner, lifework, the use of our money, friendships, vacations, home, family, business, spare time, church, and anything else the Spirit reminds us to include.

Stripped and empty, the Holy Spirit comes to cleanse and to fill us; thus are we members of His Body indeed.

> I appeal to you ... by the mercies of God, to present your bodies as a living sacrifice, holy and acceptable to God, which is your spiritual worship. Do not be conformed to this world, but be transformed by the renewal of your mind, that you may prove what is the will of God, what is good and acceptable and perfect.
>
> Romans 12:1, 2 RSV

> Although he was a Son, he learned obedience through what he suffered; and being made perfect he became the source of eternal salvation to all who obey him.
>
> Hebrews 5:8, 9 RSV

Questions and Answers

QUESTION: Will you define "the spirit of worldliness"?

ANSWER: 1 John 2:15, 16 (TLB) says it all: "Stop loving this evil world and all that it offers you, for when you love these things you show that you do not really love God; for all these worldly things, these evil desires—the craze for sex, the ambition to buy everything that appeals to you, and the pride that comes from wealth and importance—these are not from God. They are from this evil world itself." (Read the seventeenth verse, too.)

QUESTION: Define "hating your life."

ANSWER: This paradox, or apparent contradiction, in the teachings of Jesus is understandable when one is taught of the Spirit.

1. To love myself means to accept myself, to believe in myself, to believe I am loved because God loves me and furthermore to think and act like it.

2. The decision to love my life and lose it or to hate my life and keep it for eternity (in the context of John 12:24–26) seems to mean the same thing Saint Paul meant when he wrote: "But whatever gain I had, I counted as loss for the sake of Christ. Indeed I count everything as loss because of the surpassing worth of knowing Christ Jesus my Lord. For his sake I have suffered the loss of all things, and count them as refuse, in order that I may gain Christ" (Philippians 3:7, 8 RSV). He gave up everything that he counted worthwhile and counted it "refuse," or garbage, in order to be one with Christ.

Chapter Review

1. Check out, in your own life, the three hindrances Sister Therese spoke on that block God's power.
2. Discuss the difference between a total commitment to Jesus Christ and a total commitment to a holy life.
3. List the things personal commitment means to you now; add things you have feared or avoided. Test them by: Whom are you pleasing, God or man?
4. Pray the prayer of commitment, be the grain of wheat that falls into the ground.
5. The freedom Jesus is giving you through this commitment will not keep problems away—you may have more—but you will have greater ability to love and to wait for His word to you.

> ... they who wait for the Lord
>   shall renew their strength,
> they shall mount up with wings
>   like eagles,
> they shall run and not be weary,
> they shall walk and not faint.
>   Isaiah 40:31 RSV

12

By the Holy Spirit,
Who Gives Us
Ears to Hear

When you ask for and receive the fullness of God's Holy Spirit, you are more willing to hear and to respond to God's voice. The reason for this is in the heart preparation and personal commitment required, for the Holy Spirit does not fill an unclean vessel or one unwilling to wait upon Him for instructions.

Most people have reservations about the Holy Spirit and the terms various church groups use, like *baptism, filling, born again,* and so on. So did I.

One thing I'm sure of: We confuse ourselves with the semantics we use, while the Lord God wishes to draw us all together in love, into one Body, giving and receiving from one another. Terms appear harsh and unyielding, while persons we know who use these various terms are human, warm, and loving.

In my ministry, which has taken me into every denomination, I have heard so many wonderful testimonies that I know it is impossible to catalog or cubbyhole the Holy Spirit.

Humans may, however, drop their prejudices and pride and be cleansed and delivered and anointed by the Holy Spirit, so they may love one another without total agreement.

My Hindering Hang-Ups

I'd read what the Gospels say about John's baptism and Jesus' baptism, but the teaching of my church was pretty strong. Because of the emphasis on holiness in that church I attended during my teens, I have much to thank God for. Holiness of heart and life were stressed, but it seemed to me as time went on that more importance was given to outward, worldly things than to the fruits and gifts of the Spirit, which have their roots in the heart.

My chief hang-ups were pride and prejudice. To willingly face up to those two culprits took both time and inner healing. I did not want further legalism, which was part of that denomination which taught the "baptism of the Spirit" before the renewal going on today.

During the past ten years the Holy Spirit has jumped over all denominational lines, and God's power has fallen upon both Protestants and Catholics in revival measure. That settled my prejudices.

My next hang-up was the subject of glossolalia, which involved my pride in being willing to say a lot of foolish words that seemingly had no meaning or purpose.

My story has already been told in my book published in 1979, *Ask Me, Lord, I Want to Say Yes*. God in His wisdom places me right in the midst of Spirit-baptized Episcopalians, Lutherans, and Catholics who invited me to lead workshops on conversational prayer, because they wanted to learn to pray aloud together. I saw the miracle of commitment, of holiness, of simplicity and rejoiced at the great renewal taking place.

As I opened my heart for the Lord to continue to speak to me and to teach me, it was like a revelation when I finally saw it all. Unknowingly, I had received both the new birth and the baptism of the Spirit at my conversion. Both the fruits of the Spirit and some of the gifts of the Spirit began to be apparent.

The gift of tongues was missing, but then so were many of the others. Later on, I deduced from that, that if you do not wish to receive a certain gift, it is not given. God will wait until you are ready.

How did my last gift finally come? A friend of mine heard me pray in a "prayer language," when I did not know I was doing it! Later, when I was told, I could hardly believe it! How long had I been doing that?

How wise God is. Now I could never tell anyone how to do what I had done; it was a gift given to me. Since then I've heard and met others who have had the same experience.

The Release of the Spirit

How many of our prejudices would dissolve, readying us for a great spiritual ministry of love, if we had open ears to hear the instructions of the Lord!

I pray that, whatever your past experience or your hang-ups, you will begin to trust the deep, deep love of Jesus to lead you into the freedom of giving the Holy Spirit free rein in your life.

Believe that Jesus will be glorified through it all. Your motives will be cleared up, your hang-ups dissolved, and you will hear the voice within you saying, *This is the way, walk ye in it.*

If the terms used, the semantics, the words *baptism, sanctification, holiness, born again,* or whatever, still offend you (but if you are a lover of the Lord Jesus and believe in Him) it might help you if you would use the term many of us are using now, for we recognize it to be true. We refer to *the release of the Spirit,* meaning that, by your consent and commitment, you open every part of your being, and the Spirit who is within you will be released to control, fill, and guide you. Personally, I like that term. I pray that the Spirit may be released within you, to speak to you, to bring forth His gifts and His fruit.

Ask and you shall receive:

> If you then, who are evil, know how to give good gifts to your children, how much more will the heavenly Father give the Holy Spirit to those who ask him!
>
> Luke 11:13 RSV

In your asking and seeking, remember that when you gave your heart to Jesus, you got all of Him—that included the Father, the Son, and the Holy Spirit—for He never comes in pieces: He is one God. But ask yourself: How much of me did Jesus get? He wants all of you.

In the early history of the young church, hands were laid on people to receive the baptism of the Spirit. God still honors this practice, and it does aid one's faith and commitment.

Examining Your Motives

A total devotion to Jesus Christ Himself is of prime importance, and only the Holy Spirit within you can thus exalt Jesus.

Examine your motives for wanting the fullness of the Holy Spirit, the baptism. Do you want to have more power? to belong to a special group? to be "used in the Lord's service"? for deliverance from sin? to be in full-time religious work? to possess certain gifts?

God permitted me to seek a long time before I got my motives straightened out. But it was a wonderful process of heart cleansing. All my motives came under His scrutiny. I began to know what Paul was writing about in the fourth chapter of Philippians.

My Prayers and God's Answers

MY REQUEST: Lord, I need power to help others, in healing, in answered prayer, in teaching, in counseling.

HIS ANSWER:	My child, the power you need will be there just at the time you need it; this is the work of My Spirit.
MY REQUEST:	Lord, I want to be used as I see others being used.
HIS ANSWER:	My child, the gifts to help others are given by My Spirit. Your motive could be laced with pride. Let the Holy Spirit control you and give to you the gifts He wants you to have. Then Jesus will be uplifted and others drawn to Him.
MY REQUEST:	Lord, I'd like to be victorious over my besetting sin.
HIS ANSWER:	My child, the Holy Spirit will cleanse you, humble you, and put new motives within you, but your chief motive must be obedience and heart union with Jesus.

Questions and Answers for Discussion

QUESTION:	It is apparent that some of God's children possess a greater amount of the power and the presence of the Holy Spirit than do others. What makes the difference?
ANSWER:	The Spirit gives as He will. We are only recipients. Maturity may make the difference.
QUESTION:	Can one possess the Holy Spirit in minimum and maximum quantities?

ANSWER: If you are asking if one can receive more of the Holy Spirit than another, my answer is that you are confusing the issue by words. You received the Spirit when you were born again, but how much of *you* did the Spirit receive? Now you are ready to give Him more of yourself, with your full consent, and enjoy His fullness.

QUESTION: How do I give more of myself? by hearing? by obeying? by asking?

ANSWER: Read again the chapters that spoke to you about obedience and commitment. There needs to be an emptying, a searching, even a sorrow for withholding yourself for so long—a longing, a need, and confession of sin. On the other hand, as soon as hands are laid on for the release of the Spirit in His fullness, some receive immediately and the whole searching time comes afterwards.

Your commitment: It helps to be specific when you lay yourself and all you have at the feet of Jesus. Visualize laying the following on God's altar to be consumed: yourself, your ambitions, your family, your lifework, your life partner, your money, your church, your friends, your pleasures, even your failures. If there is anything else, it will be revealed to you.

QUESTION: What is the difference between the terms *the baptism of the Spirit* and *the filling of the Spirit?*

ANSWER: The baptism of the Spirit, for many, is a one-time experience. The filling of the Spirit can take place many times.

QUESTION: My biggest hang-up is still the question regarding tongues. Do all who receive the baptism of the Spirit speak in tongues? Isn't that only one of the many gifts spoken of in 1 Corinthians 12?

ANSWER: No, all do not receive the gift of tongues (or the prayer language) at the time of baptism. Some receive it later, some never do. Yes, the gift of tongues is the last of the gifts mentioned. Paul gives instructions on how to use this gift and how not to use it. To receive the fullness of the Giver is more important than to receive any of His gifts.

QUESTION: Isn't speaking in tongues the sign that a person has received the baptism?

ANSWER: For many this is true, but I agree with Catherine Marshall that *love* is the chief sign. Love is the fruit of the Spirit from which all the other graces flow. All other signs will pass away, but love will remain forever (1 Corinthians 13).

QUESTION: My readers ask if I have received this gift.

ANSWER: Yes, but not until years later. Many other gifts were given first.

QUESTION: Some have asked how I use this gift of the prayer language.

ANSWER: In intercession and praise. When I am praying for another and don't know what to pray for, when English words run out, as well as the few Chinese words I know, the prayer language seems to express the worship, praise, and thanksgiving my mind cannot express.

QUESTION: Some Spirit-baptized people are more gifted than others. On what basis are these gifts given?

ANSWER: Turn to 1 Corinthians 12 for the answer. The Holy Spirit makes known to us and leads us into the gifts He knows are for the common good:

1. Gifts are given to help the entire church (1 Corinthians 12:7).
2. Gifts are given by decision of the Spirit (1 Corinthians 12:11).
3. We are all given different gifts to make the Body of Christ complete (Romans 12:4, 5).
4. Gifts are given so that God's people will be built up to strength and maturity and be filled with Christ, becoming more like Him, so the whole body is healthy and full of love.

QUESTION: What is the difference between the gifts
            and the fruits of the Spirit?

ANSWER: Briefly, the fruits of the Spirit are personal
            character qualities, while the gifts of the
            Spirit are for the edification and building
            up of the whole body of believers or the
            church.

I have yet many things to say to you, but you
cannot bear them now. When the Spirit of truth
comes . . . He will glorify me, for he will take what
is mine and declare it to you.

John 16:12–14 RSV

But we have this treasure in earthen vessels, to
show that the transcendent power belongs to God
and not to us.

2 Corinthians 4:7 RSV

He who has ears to hear, let him hear.

Appendix

The Scriptures Speak

Prepared by Connie Warren

Minister to One Another in Love

The charge to love one another in the Epistles (Romans 13:8) echoes Jesus' message in the Gospels, "A new commandment I give to you, that you love one another; even as I have loved you . . ." (John 13:34 RSV). This love-one-another theme weaves its way through the Old and New Testaments, imbedding in our hearts and minds the Lord's divine intention that humankind live in harmony with one another.

But God did not leave us to our own inadequate devices to achieve this life-style. Rather He wisely tucked into Scripture profound guidelines, which through His power, secure our adequacy. We launch the love-one-another course of action by being devoted to God (Matthew 22:37), seeking Him daily (Psalms 5:3), and listening to Him as He speaks to us (John 10:4).

Love one another—the Scriptures speak and tell us how:

151

Worship With One Another
Worship in spirit and in truth (John 4:23, 24)
Partake of the Lord's Supper together (Acts 2:42)
Read the Scriptures together (1 Timothy 4:13)
Teach and admonish one another with psalms, hymns, and spiritual songs (Colossians 3:16)
Pray for one another (Matthew 18:19, 20)

Care for the Spiritual Needs of One Another
Minister to one another with spiritual gifts (1 Corinthians 12:4–12; 14:26; 1 Peter 4:10)
Be devoted to one another (Romans 12:10)
Confess faults or sins to one another (James 5:16)
Forgive one another (Colossians 3:13)
Pray for one another (James 5:16)

Meet the Physical Needs of One Another
Provide clothing, food, and shelter (Matthew 25:35; Hebrews 13:2)
Share our material possessions with one another (Acts 4:32; 2 Corinthians 8:1–5)
Contribute to the needs of God's people (Romans 12:13)

Encourage One Another
Care for one another (1 Corinthians 12:25, 26)
Build up (or edify) one another with spiritual gifts (1 Corinthians 14:26)
Encourage one another (1 Thessalonians 5:11; Hebrews 10:25)

Stimulate one another to love and to good deeds (Hebrews 10:24)

Live in Servant Heartedness With One Another
Wash one another's feet (John 13:14; 1 Timothy 5:10)
Regard others as more important than oneself (Philippians 2:3)
Give preference to one another (Romans 12:10)
Look out for the interests of one another (Philippians 2:4)
Be subject to one another (Ephesians 5:21)
Serve one another with our spiritual gifts (Romans 12:8)

Open Your Hearts and Homes to One Another
Be devoted to one another (Romans 12:10)
Meet together (Hebrews 10:25)
Fellowship with one another (Acts 2:42)
Be hospitable to one another (1 Peter 4:9; Hebrews 13:1, 2)
Eat some of our meals together (Acts 2:46)
Share our Christian pilgrimages with one another (2 Corinthians 1:3, 4)
Live in peace with one another (1 Thessalonians 5:13)

To hear and adhere to these guideposts in Scripture is to aim at Christlikeness in our relationships with others, for all are visible in Jesus. In so doing, we have heeded Jesus' greatest commandment: "You shall love the Lord your God with all your heart, and with all your soul, and with all your mind . . . You shall love your neighbor as yourself" (Matthew 22:37, 39 RSV). The results are fourfold.

1. The lives of our neighbors are enriched because of our sincere love for them.
2. We find personal fulfillment in self-giving, and Christ-centered self-esteem soars within us ("love . . . yourself").
3. Jesus is made visible to the world, because His light radiates within us. "A new commandment I give to you, that you love one another. . . . *By this all men will know you are my disciples . . .*" (John 13:34, 35 RSV, *italics mine*). "You are the light of the world . . ." (Matthew 5:14 RSV).
4. We have truly *loved the Lord our God*—"Truly, I say to you, as you did it to . . . the least of these my brethren, you did it to me" (Matthew 25:40).

Loving one another, a most rewarding biblical precept, makes the Kingdom of God *come alive* on earth today. The scriptural love-one-another guidelines can be accomplished, even under persecution, in homes and in churches. As Mother Teresa says, "I am a distributor of the Lord's compassion."

Bibliography

Cunningham, Loren. *Is That Really You, God?* P.O. Box YWAM, Kailua, Kona Hawaii, 96740.

Copeland, Gloria. *God's Will for You.* Fort Worth, Tex.: Kenneth Copeland Pubs., 1972.

Glasser, William, M.D. *Reality Therapy.* New York: Harper & Row, 1965.

Harris, Thomas A. *I'm OK—You're OK: A Practical Guide to Transactional Analysis,* New York: Harper & Row, 1969.

Murphree, Jon T. *When God Says You're OK: A Christian Approach to Transactional Analysis.* Downers Grove, Ill: Inter-Varsity Press, 1975.

New Covenant Magazine, P.O. Box 7009, Ann Arbor, Michigan 48107.

Rinker, Rosalind. *Ask Me Lord, I Want To Say Yes.* So. Plainfield, N.J.: Bridge Pub., 1979.

Sheik, Madame Bilquis. *I Dared to Call Him Father.* Lincoln, Va.: Chosen Books, 1981.

Stapleton, Ruth C. *The Experience of Inner Healing.* Waco, Tex.: Word Books, 1979.

Stapleton, Ruth C. *The Gift of Inner Healing.* Waco, Tex.: Word Books, 1976.